BRAIN GA...

CSI

CRIME SCENE INVESTIGATION

pil

Publications International, Ltd.

Puzzle creators: Cihan Altay, Helem An, Jim Bumgardner, Keith Burns, Myles Callum, Philip Carter, Andrew Clarke, Barry Clarke, Gino Collins, Caroline Delbert, Harvey Estes, Josie Faulkner, Adrian Fisher, Erich Friedman, Luke Haward, Shelly Hazard, Naomi Lipsky, David Millar, Michael Moreci, Elsa Neal, Planet-x-Graphix, Stephen Ryder, Gianni Sarcone, Paul Seaburn, Terry Stickels, Nicole Sulgit, Wayne Robert Williams, Alex Willmore

Puzzle illustrators: Helem An, Caroline Delbert, Chris Gattorna, Pat Hagle, Robin Humer, Nick LaShure, Shavan R. Spears, Jen Torche

Louis Weber, CEO
Publications International, Ltd.
8140 Lehigh Avenue
Morton Grove, IL 60053

Permission is never granted for commercial purposes.

ISBN: 978-1-68022-777-2

Manufactured in China.

8 7 6 5 4 3 2 1

IT'S TIME TO SOLVE!

If you've marveled at the sharp eyes, dogged investigative skills, and scientific advances that allow people to solve crimes, now it's your turn! In *Brain Games®: Crime Scene Investigation*, you'll find an assortment of puzzles that will test your skills. Crime-scene themed puzzles will let you combine your love of puzzles with your love of crime stories. Plus we've included visual puzzles to train your eyes to spot small details, memory puzzles to sharpen your visual memory, logic puzzles to enhance your reasoning skills, and more. If you're stuck, just turn to the answer key at the back for a hint.

So if you love forensics, fingerprints, and fun, turn the page and start your investigation!

FROM CLUES TO TRIAL

Change just one letter on each line to go from the top word to the bottom word. Do not change the order of the letters. You must have a common English word at each step.

CLUES

———

———

———

———

———

TRIAL

COME TOGETHER

Set each of the tile sets into the empty spaces below to create 3 nine-letter words related to investigation. Each tile set is used only once.

T I C   S U S   T E D

B A L   E X A   L I S

M I N   E R S   P E C

Answers on page 175.

CRIME STINKS

Change just one letter on each line to go from the top word to the bottom word. Do not change the order of the letters. You must have a common English word at each step.

CRIME

_____

_____

_____

_____

_____

_____

STINK

CRIME RHYMES

Each clue leads to a 2-word answer that rhymes, such as BIG PIG or STABLE TABLE. The numbers in parentheses after the clue give the number of letters in each word. For example, "cookware taken from the oven (3, 3)" would be "hot pot."

1. Theft of a sushi ingredient (3, 5): _____

2. Fingerprint found at a cheese store robbery (4, 4): _____

3. Shoplifter from a butcher (4, 5): _____

4. Citrus-related robbery (4, 5): _____

5. Robber of drinks (8, 5): _____

6. Plans to steal boat (5, 4): _____

7. Thoughtful investigator (10, 9): _____

8. Foot impression found in the herbal garden (4, 5): _____

Answers on page 175.

CRIME CRYPTOGRAM

Cryptograms are messages in substitution code. Break the code to read the message. For example, THE SMART CAT might become FVO QWGDF JGF if **F** is substituted for **T, V** for **H, O** for **E,** and so on.

ZNK GIZUX'Y IUYZGX GIIAYKJ NOS UL G
JGYZGXJRE IXOSK, HAZ ZNK VUROIK XKLAYKJ ZU
OTBKYZOMGZK. CNGZ JOJ NK JU?

NK YZURK ZNK YIKTK!

MEALTIME CRIME

Cryptograms are messages in substitution code. Break the code to read the message. For example, THE SMART CAT might become FVO QWGDF JGF if **F** is substituted for **T, V** for **H, O** for **E,** and so on.

ZKDW GLG WKH KHDGOLQH UHDG IRU WKH
EDNHUB WKHIW WKDW WRRN SODFH GXULQJ WKH
VROVWLFH LQ MXQH?

WKH VXPPHUWLPH NHB OLPH FULPH.

Answers on page 175.

MOTEL HIDEOUT

A thief hides out in one of the 45 motel rooms listed in the chart below. The motel's in-house detective received a sheet of four clues, signed "The Holiday Thief." Using these clues, the detective found the room number within 15 minutes—but by that time, the thief had fled. Can you find the thief's motel room quicker?

1. It is a prime number larger than 20.
2. The second digit is larger than the first.
3. The second digit is divisible by three.
4. The first digit is not divisible by 2.

51	52	53	54	55	56	57	58	59
41	42	43	44	45	46	47	48	49
31	32	33	34	35	36	37	38	39
21	22	23	24	25	26	27	28	29
11	12	13	14	15	16	17	18	19

Answers on page 175.

TYPES OF EVIDENCE (PART I)

Just walk through a room, let alone commit a crime, and you'll leave a trace that will detail your every action. Read the information below about forensic evidence, then turn to page 10.

1. **Tool marks:** If you use any sort of object to commit your crime—a pickax on a door lock, a ladder to reach a window, a knife or a rag (for any purpose)—it will be traceable. Tools used in any capacity create tiny nicks that can be detected, identified, and tracked by a crime scene investigator.

2. **Paint:** A paint chip left at a crime scene reveals volumes. If it's from the vehicle you used in committing the crime, it indicates the make and model. If paint is found on the tool you used to break into a house, it could place you at the scene. Think it's too hard to distinguish specific paint colors? There are 40,000 types of paint classified in police databases.

3. **Broken glass:** Microscopic glass fragments cling to your clothes and can't be laundered out easily. Crime labs examine tint, thickness, density, and refractive index of the fragments to determine their origins.

4. **Dust and dirt:** Even if you're a neat-and-tidy sort of criminal, dust and dirt are often missed by the most discerning eye. These particles can reveal where you live and work and if you have a pet (and what kind). If you've trudged through fields or someone's backyard, researchers can use palynology—the science that studies plant spores, insects, seeds, and other microorganisms—to track you down.

5. **Fibers:** The sources include clothing, drapes, wigs, carpets, furniture, blankets, pets, and plants. Using a compound microscope, an analyst can determine if the fibers are manufactured or natural, which often indicates their value as evidence. The more specific the fiber, the easier it will be to identify (consider the differences between fibers from a white cotton T-shirt and those from a multicolored wool sweater). There are more than a thousand known fibers, as well as several thousand dyes, so if an exact match is found, you will be too.

6. **Blood:** A victim's blood tells investigators a lot, but they're also looking for different kinds of blood—including yours if you were injured at the scene—and the patterns of blood distribution. Detectives are well trained in collecting blood evidence to estimate when the crime occurred and who was involved. By the way, don't bother to clean up any blood, because investigators use special lights that reveal your efforts.

7. **Bodily fluids:** Saliva, urine, vomit, and semen are a crime-scene investigator's dream, providing DNA evidence that will implicate even the most savvy criminal. Saliva is commonly found left behind by a criminal who took time out for a beverage, a snack, or a cigarette.

8. **Fingerprints:** One of the best ways to identify a criminal is through fingerprints left at the scene. But you kept track of what you touched and then wiped everything down, right? It doesn't matter: You still left smeared prints that can be lifted and analyzed. Investigators enter fingerprint evidence into national databases that can point directly to you.

9. **Shoe prints:** If you have feet (and assuming you're not a "barefoot burglar"), you left behind shoe prints. They could be in soil or snow or perhaps on a carpet or across a bare floor. The particular treads on the soles of shoes make them easy to trace, and the bottoms of most shoes have nicks or scratches that make them easy to identify.

10. **Hair:** Humans shed a lot of hair from all parts of their bodies, so bald bandits have no advantage. Hairs as tiny as eyelashes and eyebrows have unique characteristics that reveal a lot about a person, including race, dietary habits, and overall health. And don't forget: While your hair is dropping all over the crime scene, the victim's hair is clinging to your clothing.

TYPES OF EVIDENCE (PART II)

(Do not read this until you have read the previous pages!)

1. There are 40,000 types of paint classified in police databases.

☐ **TRUE** ☐ **FALSE**

2. The study of fibers is called palynology.

☐ **TRUE** ☐ **FALSE**

3. Investigators can only lift perfect fingerprints.

☐ **TRUE** ☐ **FALSE**

4. A bald criminal could still be convicted on evidence of hair.

☐ **TRUE** ☐ **FALSE**

5. Broken glass cannot easily be laundered out of clothes.

☐ **TRUE** ☐ **FALSE**

Answers on page 175.

BURIED DIAMONDS

The thief has buried stolen diamonds in various locations and left a list as a memory aid; however, she mixed up the list. Although each item is in the correct column, only one item in each column is correctly positioned. The following facts are true about the correct order:

1. River is two places above dogwood and three places above 7 diamonds.

2. Neither lake nor wood are fifth.

3. The 10 diamonds amount is one place below beech and one place above lake.

4. Fifth place is occupied by neither 10 nor 15 diamonds.

5. Neither ash nor elm is second.

6. The 8 diamonds amount is one place below garden and three places above fir.

Can you give the tree, location, and number of diamonds buried for each position?

	Tree	Location	No. Diamonds
1	ash	park	5
2	beech	garden	7
3	cedar	river	8
4	dogwood	wood	10
5	elm	fence	12
6	fir	lake	15

Answers on page 175.

QUICK CRIME QUIZ

1. Long before they were used to identify criminals, fingerprints were some-times used to "sign" documents in lieu of a signature.

☐ **TRUE**   ☐ **FALSE**

2. In Mark Twain's books "Life on the Mississippi" and "Pudd'n Head Wilson," these were used to identify perpetrators of crimes.

☐ **HAIR**   ☐ **FINGERPRINTS**   ☐ **FOOTPRINTS**

3. The Bertillion method, named after the French police officer who invented it, used body measurements to establish identity.

☐ **TRUE**   ☐ **FALSE**

4. Bertillion was also the first person to standardize the use of:

☐ **DNA TESTING**   ☐ **MUG SHOTS**

5. America's first detective agency, the Pinkertons, was created in this year.

☐ **1850**   ☐ **1912**

Answers on page 175.

CRIMINALS

How many kinds of criminals can you find here? We count 8. To spell out a criminal, keep moving from one letter to the next in any direction—up, down, across, or diagonally. You may move in several different directions for each word. You can also use letters more than once—but not in the same word.

M O B B O O
T U R E R K
B L G G T C
R A G S I H
W I N D E F

COUNT CASHULA

Count Cashula, the world's greatest money magician, was about to perform his grand finale. He had already performed many amazing monetary feats, including turning blank paper into currency, bending a quarter with his bare hands, and convincing a concession clerk to give him change for a hundred. Now he would prove that no one in the audience knew how to count money. Count Cashula gave each audience member a pen, paper, and the following instruction: "Quickly write down this number: Twelve thousand twelve hundred and twenty-two dollars." When they held up their papers for Count Cashula to see, amazingly all of them had written down the wrong number. Why?

Answers on page 175.

MEDICAL EXAMINERS

Every name listed is contained within the group of letters. Names can be found in a straight line horizontally, vertically, or diagonally. They may be read either forward or backward.

AL ROBBINS (CSI: Crime Scene Investigation)

ALEXX WOODS (CSI: Miami)

CAMILLE SAROYAN (Bones)

DAVID PHILLIPS (CSI: Crime Scene Investigation)

ELIZABETH RODGERS (Law and Order franchise)

EVE LOCKHART (Waking the Dead)

FELIX GIBSON (Waking the Dead)

FRANKIE WHARTON (Waking the Dead)

GERALD JACKSON (NCIS)

JIMMY PALMER (NCIS)

JORDAN CAVANAUGH (Crossing Jordan)

JULIANNA COX (Homicide)

KAY SCARPETTA (Patricia Cornwell's book series)

LORETTA WADE (NCIS: New Orleans)

MAURA ISLES (Rizzoli and Isles)

MAX BERGMAN (Hawaii Five-O)

MELINDA WARNER (Law and Order: SVU)

QUINCY (Quincy, M.E.)

ROSE SCHWARTZ (NCIS: Los Angeles)

```
L M K C A M I L L E S A R O Y A N
N O S N K A Y S C A R P E T T A D
O F R E N O S K C A J D L A R E G
T O T E L X O C A N N A I L U J Y
R R A G T S F Y F L E K Z D P C C
A L A L L T I M S Q V J A U G M H
H L W H H Q A A A B G X B F S E G
W N E A K B U W R X K H E E P L U
E P P X B C F I A U B R T L V I A
I N Y E X P O P N D A E H I X N N
K Z U R W W Q L M C E M R X G D A
N A J H I N O T E P Y L O G F A V
A L B O N Y E O Q V S A D I M W A
R R E T O A K N D A E P G B M A C
F O D E E X G C O S H Y E S D R N
J B C S Z X G E G O Y M R O Q N A
S B L P H W E I M V Y M S N D E D
Y I S P I L L I H P D I V A D R R
T N P G J D Q P Q R O J F D X B O
Y S Q R O S E S C H W A R T Z L J
```

Answers on page 175.

FINGERPRINT MATCH

There are six sets of fingerprints. Find each match.

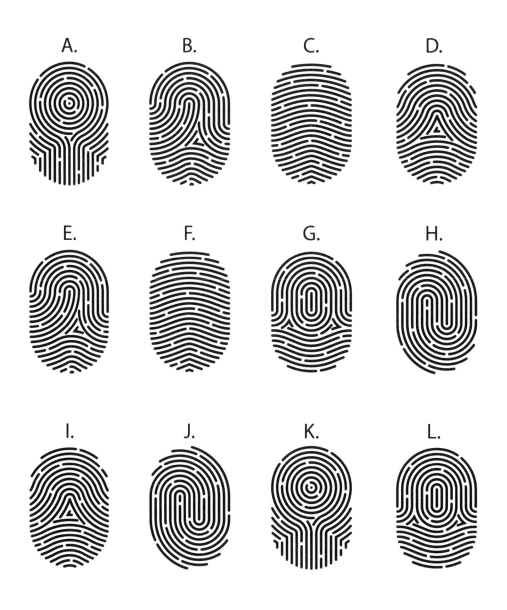

16

Answers on page 176.

WHAT DO YOU SEE? (PART 1)

Study this picture of the crime scene for 1 minute, then turn the page.

WHAT DO YOU SEE? (PART II)

(Do not read this until you have read the previous page!)

1. The victim's purse was:

☐ **OPEN**   ☐ **CLOSED**

2. One of the victim's shoes had fallen off.

☐ **TRUE**   ☐ **FALSE**

3. This piece of furniture was at the left side of the scene.

☐ **CHEST OF DRAWERS**   ☐ **DRESSING TABLE**

4. The victim's phone was found near this hand:

☐ **LEFT HAND**   ☐ **RIGHT HAND**

5. Was there a set of keys anywhere in the scene?

☐ **YES**   ☐ **NO**

Answers on page 176.

STRINGING ALONG

Crime scene investigators have to think creatively! Read the following story and see if you can puzzle out the answe.

It was lunchtime, and Hector finished the last bite of his sandwich. Linda, the newest member of the office staff, was with him at the corner table at Curly's Bar & Grill.

"They tell me you're something of a practical joker," said Linda. "I was hesitant to join you for lunch."

"No practical jokes. I just collect puzzles that are tough to figure out."

"Will you show me, Hector?" Linda asked eagerly. "I just love puzzles!"

"For you, Linda, I will perform one of my favorites. But you'll have to excuse me first."

Hector walked over to the bar, then returned with a piece of string and a pair of scissors.

Linda looked perplexed.

"May I have your empty coffee cup, please?" Hector asked with a theatrical flair. He tied one end of the string to the handle and lifted the other end so the coffee cup was dangling in midair.

Hector continued, "The object of this little trick is to cut the string near the middle without letting the cup fall to the table. Don't touch the cup or allow it to rest anywhere."

Linda looked at the cup hanging on the piece of string. "Go ahead and show me, Hector. It looks impossible but I'm sure there's a logical solution."

HOW DID HECTOR CUT THE STRING
WITHOUT MAKING THE CUP FALL?

Answers on page 176.

LOGIC: THE MORNING LANDSCAPE

After a local landscaper disappeared, investigators tried to trace his morning route from his notes. They found that he had received orders for 4 trees: an apple, an elm, a maple, and a pear. The 4 customers were the Browns, the Greens, the Greys, and the Whites. Oddly, the addresses of the 4 customers had the same names as the trees he had to deliver: Apple Lane, Elm Drive, Maple Lane, and Pear Drive. Using the information collected from his notes, determine the order in which the deliveries were made, in whose yard each tree was planted, and on what street. Who did he see last?

1. The Grey family does not live on Apple Lane.

2. No tree was planted on a street bearing its name, but one fruit tree was planted on a street bearing the name of the other fruit tree.

3. The landscaper planted the maple tree later than he planted a tree at the Browns' house but earlier than he planted a tree at either address followed by the word drive.

4. He did not plant the pear tree on a street followed by the word lane, but he planted it before his stop at the White's house.

	APPLE TREE	ELM TREE	MAPLE TREE	PEAR TREE	APPLE LANE	ELM DRIVE	MAPLE LANE	PEAR DRIVE	BROWN	GREEN	GREY	WHITE
FIRST												
SECOND												
THIRD												
FOURTH												
APPLE LANE												
ELM DRIVE												
MAPLE LANE												
PEAR DRIVE												
BROWN												
GREEN												
GREY												
WHITE												

Answers on page 176.

SEARCHING FOR EVIDENCE

ACROSS

1. Guitarist at Woodstock
5. Cabinet department
10. Dieter's choice
14. Declare as true
15. National rival
16. Egg on
17. Phobia start
18. Baseball squads
19. Regatta squad
20. The crime took place in New York City at the _____
23. Buddhism type
24. Century 21's field
25. AARP member, often
29. New Age singer of "Orinoco Flow"
31. Where the victim was forced to take a _____ drug
33. More ready to be picked
38. Put down
39. Trap
41. Ankle-length 68-Across
42. "Let's hear _____ our next contestant"
44. Right before being _____
46. Running track shape
48. Lorraine neighbor
49. Drill sergeant's instruction
53. Heat organization: abbr.
54. By a woman wearing _____
59. "The doctor _____"
60. Renter's paper
61. Multipatient hospital room
64. Lead-in for Romeo
65. Rarin' to go
66. Lots
67. States
68. Woman's garment
69. Not-quite-final program version

DOWN

1. Airline code for a Florida city
2. "_____ had it up to here!"
3. Desktop bar
4. Pressing need?
5. Camping lights
6. Man in the moon?
7. Reception performers
8. Portent
9. Prayer beads
10. St. _____ (Caribbean island)
11. Swashbuckling Flynn
12. Ticket seller
13. Filled with gossip
21. Its logo was a green alligator
22. Rip
25. Protection purchase, perhaps: abbr.
26. Q.E.D. word: Lat.
27. Babe in the woods
28. _____ -European
29. Modern letter: hyph.
30. Geek
32. '60s teen idol Paul
34. Little devils
35. John Phillips was one
36. Co. man
37. Hitchhiker's hope
40. Facilitators
43. Parks on a bus
45. Jai _____
47. Kind of threat
49. Opera parts
50. Unit with T as its symbol
51. Enlighten
52. Pavlova and others
53. They might smell a rat
55. King with three daughters
56. Beep
57. Q-tip, e.g.

58. Can't stand
62. Decompose
63. The crime was solved by finding traces of _____ contained in each theme answer of 20-, 31-, 44-, and 54-Across

1	2	3	4		5	6	7	8	9		10	11	12	13
14					15						16			
17					18						19			
		20		21					22					
				23				24						
25	26	27	28			29	30							
31					32				33	34	35	36	37	
38				39			40		41					
42			43		44			45						
		46	47				48							
49	50	51	52			53								
54				55	56			57	58					
59				60					61		62	63		
64				65					66					
67				68					69					

Answers on page 176.

REMEMBERING THE SCENE (PART I)

You will be grilled on the witness stand for your testimony in the case, and you'll want to answer each question promptly, accurately, and thoroughly. Read over your case notes, then turn to page 26 and see how much you remember.

The burglary and assault took place on Monday morning, March 14. The homeowner, Daniel J. Farsnooth, had been knocked out by burglars when he returned home after his morning run, interrupting the in-progress burglary. They subsequently fled the scene of the crime.

Farsnooth lives alone. He has owned the house for three years. He runs regularly at the same time every morning (leaving his house approximately 6:30 AM, returning 7:15 AM, before leaving again for work at 8 AM).

There was blood (Farsnooth's) in the foyer in three different locations.

An umbrella stand had been knocked over in the struggle.

Three hairs were found that might belong to the robbers.

One partial muddy shoeprint had been left on the entryway rug; it did not match any of the shoes in Farsnooth's closet, but he had had friends over on Sunday for a barbecue and said it could have been left on Sunday.

According to Farsnooth, all missing items in the house had been taken from the living room. He listed the following items as stolen: one DVD player; 3 DVDs (*The Martian; Star Wars: The Force Awakens; Captain America: Civil War*); stack of mail, including a credit card application and multiple ads; decorative clock, approximate value $75-100; one laptop. The TV had been moved to the edge of its stand.

According to Farsnooth, the front door was closed but probably not locked when he returned to the house after running. He went to unlock it automatically, but he noted that the door did not open when he did so, and he had to try again. This led him to believe later that it had been unlocked and was the point of entry for the thieves. There were no other signs of forced entry at any of the doors.

He had not seen anything out of place when he approached the house. There was no car parked in his driveway. There were multiple cars parked in the street, but he noted none that seemed out of place. He did not remember specifics about any of the cars on the street.

When he entered the house, he heard voices and saw two people wearing black ski masks, dressed in black, rushing at him. After a scuffle, one of them hit him on the head, and he fell down. The robbers ran past him through the open front door and fled on foot. He heard a car start up shortly afterward. He identified their voices as male, no accent. They were both of medium height and slim build.

REMEMBERING THE SCENE (PART II)

(Do not read this until you have read the previous page!)

1. How many DVDs were stolen?

     A. 1   B. 2   C. 3   D. 4

2. The TV was stolen as well.

     ☐ **TRUE**   ☐ **FALSE**

3. A partial fingerprint was found in the foyer.

     ☐ **TRUE**   ☐ **FALSE**

4. Farsnooth's wife was away on vacation when the robbers came.

     ☐ **TRUE**   ☐ **FALSE**

5. How many robbers were there?

     A. 1   B. 2   C. 3   D. Unknown

6. A clock was stolen. What was its approximate value?

     A. $10   B. $50   C. $75   D. $500

Answers on page 176.

SCIENCE

1. When is the flame of a gas stove the hottest?

   a) when it is white

   b) when it is blue

   c) when it is red

   d) when it is orange

2. What is a piece of cosmic debris on Earth called?

   a) a meteor

   b) a meteorite

   c) a satellite

   d) a moon rock

3. Bats are:

   a) extremely well sighted

   b) farsighted

   c) partially blind

   d) totally blind

4. Approximately how far is the moon from the Earth?

   a) 240,000 miles

   b) 300,000 miles

   c) 420,000 miles

   d) 510,000 miles

5. About how many hairs does the average blond-haired person have?

   a) 10,000 hairs

   b) 70,000 hairs

   c) 140,000 hairs

   d) 280,000 hairs

Answers on page 176.

WILD WEST

The Western cattle trail was notorious for murder among the cowhands. The leader noted the deaths of the 6 hands who were shot on the journey, but on reaching his destination he found that he had mixed up the order and details of those who died. Although each detail is in the correct column, only 1 entry in each of the 4 columns is correctly positioned. Can you find the correct name, surname, location, and firearm involved in each murder and determine the correct order in which the killings took place?

1. San Antonio is 3 places above the Golden Boy.

2. Hitchcock is somewhere above Lightning and 2 places above the Derringer.

3. Earp is 2 places below Fort Griffin.

4. Kid is 1 row below both Butch and Colby.

5. Fingers is immediately below Earp but 3 places below Garrett.

6. Butch is 1 row below the Winchester and somewhere above Cat.

7. The Peacemaker is 2 rows above Dodge City.

	Name	Surname	Location	Firearm
1	Abel	Garrett	San Antonio	Schofield
2	Butch	Hitchcock	Fort Griffin	Peacemaker
3	Cat	Indiana	Dodge City	Derringer
4	Drew	James	Ogallala	Cavalry
5	Earp	Kid	Colby	Winchester
6	Fingers	Lightning	Red River	Golden Boy

Answers on page 176.

SUPERMARKET SHENANIGANS

Checkout Charlie was convinced he was being cheated by the automated checkout scanner at the grocery store, so he memorized the prices of every item in the supermarket, then watched the screen as the clerk scanned the items of everyone in front of him. The man in the green shirt had a jar of applesauce and a pound of beef, which scanned correctly for a total of $5.40. The woman with the red scarf had a bag of candy and a doughnut, which scanned correctly for a total of $2.90. The man in blue shorts had a pound of beef and a carton of eggnog, which scanned correctly for a total of $7.10. The woman in the pink miniskirt had a doughnut and a jar of applesauce, which scanned correctly for a total of $3.10. The man with the purple cap had a carton of eggnog and a bag of candy, which scanned correctly for a total of $5.70. When it was Checkout Charlie's turn, he was distracted by the lovely young checkout clerk, who was wearing a multicolored top. She told him his total was $4.80, and Charlie paid without ever taking his eyes off her, so he didn't check that his 2 items had scanned correctly. Because he bought 2 items that had already been scanned, the total was correct. Which two items did love-struck Charlie buy, and how much did each of the scanned items cost?

CRACK THE PASSWORD

The criminal's files are password protected, and they will auto-delete if you enter the wrong password. But he did leave a cheat sheet, missing one letter. Can you complete the below sequence to crack the password?

RMP ___ CR

Answers on pages 176-177.

THE YELLOW-BRICK ROAD

How good are you at determining truth? The yellow-brick road splits into the blue- and red-brick roads, which lead respectively to the red city and the green city. In one of these cities, everyone tells the truth; in the other, everyone lies. You want to get to the city of truth. Two people are waiting at the fork in the road, one from each city. You can ask one person one question, and you ask this: "If I were to ask the other person which road leads to the city of truth, what would they tell me?" The person answers: "They would tell you to take the red road."

Which road should you take?

A. The red road.

B. The blue road.

C. It is impossible to say.

WORD LADDER

Can you change just one letter on each line to transform the top word to the bottom word? Don't change the order of the letters, and make sure you have a common English word at each step.

SEEK

_____ flowers grow from this

_____ what you click after writing an email

_____ repair

_____ you may change it, from time to time

FIND

Answers on page 177.

EAVESDROPPING LOGIC

You hear a commotion as you are rounding the corner of a busy street. The moment you turn the corner, you witness the following scene: A girl in roller skates is lying on the ground in some pain, and a man is standing with his bicycle by her side. An old woman has stopped in the street before them and says to the man, "You went straight into her!" To the girl, she asks, "Are you all right, dear?"

"No, no, it wasn't his fault . . . " the girl whimpers, "I ran into him at the traffic light."

"Well, that's not exactly fair" says the man....

Which of the following is the most likely end to the man's sentence?

A. "...I shouldn't have been in this part of the lane, so it was partially my fault."

B. "...I ran into you, you must have memory loss from the head injury."

C. "...It was your fault, I didn't do anything!"

D. "...Didn't you hear what this girl said? Her account it completely at odds with yours!"

Answers on page 177.

CAN A CLUE SET YOU FREE?

Change just one letter on each line to go from the top word to the bottom word. Do not change the order of the letters. You must have a common English word at each step.

CLUE

_____

_____

_____

FREE

TELL A TALE, GO TO JAIL

Change just one letter on each line to go from the top word to the bottom word. Do not change the order of the letters. You must have a common English word at each step.

TALE

_____

_____

_____

JAIL

Answers on page 177.

MOTEL HIDEOUT

A thief hides out in one of the 45 motel rooms listed in the chart below. The motel's in-house detective received a sheet of four clues, signed "The Holiday Thief." Using these clues, the detective found the room number within 15 minutes—but by that time, the thief had fled. Can you find the thief's motel room quicker?

1. The number is not divisible by four.
2. The first digit is as large or larger than the second digit.
3. The digits add up to 6.
4. The number is divisible by 6.

51	52	53	54	55	56	57	58	59
41	42	43	44	45	46	47	48	49
31	32	33	34	35	36	37	38	39
21	22	23	24	25	26	27	28	29
11	12	13	14	15	16	17	18	19

Answers on page 177.

POISON! (PART I)

Long a favorite of mystery-novel writers and opportunistic bad guys, poison has an ancient and infamous reputation. Read some facts about poison below, then turn to page 36.

POISON PLANTS

Deadly Nightshade, aka belladonna: Every part of this perennial herb is poisonous, but the berries are especially dangerous. The poison attacks the nervous system instantly, causing a rapid pulse, hallucinations, convulsions, ataxia (lack of muscle coordination) and coma.

Wolfsbane: This deadly plant was used as an arrow poison by the ancient Chinese, and its name comes from the Greek word meaning "dart." Wolfsbane takes a while to work, but when it does, it causes extreme anxiety, chest pain, and death from respiratory arrest.

Meadow Saffron: This tough little plant can be boiled and dried, and it still retains all of its poisonous power. As little as seven milligrams of this stuff could cause colic, paralysis, and heart failure.

Hemlock: This plant is probably the best known of the herbaceous poisons: It was used to knock off the Greek philosopher Socrates. Hemlock is poisonous down to the last leaf and will often send you into a coma before it finishes you for good.

GOOD OLD ARSENIC

Arsenic—colorless, tasteless, and odorless—has been called "the poison of kings" and "the king of poisons" because for hundreds of years it was the poison of choice used by members of the ruling class to murder one another.

This close relative of phosphorous exists in a variety of compounds, not all of which are poisonous. Women in Victorian times used to rub a diluted arsenic compound into their skin to improve their complexions, and some modern medications used to treat cancer actually contain arsenic. When certain arsenic compounds are concentrated, however, they're deadly; arsenic has been blamed for widespread death through groundwater contamination.

Many historians believe that Napoleon died of arsenic poisoning while imprisoned, because significant traces of arsenic were found in his body by forensics experts 200 years after his death. It has been argued, however, that at that time in history, wallpaper and paint often contained arsenic-laced pigments, and that Napoleon was simply exposed to the poison in his everyday surroundings.

Emerald green, a color of paint used by Impressionist painters, contained an arsenic-based pigment. Some historians suggest that Van Gogh's neurological problems had a great deal to do with his use of large quantities of emerald green paint.

Even one of history's best and brightest minds, Leonardo da Vinci, dabbled with chemical weapons. The artist, and sometime inventor of war machines, proposed to "throw poison in the form of powder upon galleys." He stated, "Chalk, fine sulfide of arsenic, and powdered verdigris [toxic copper acetate] may be thrown among enemy ships by means of small mangonels [single-arm catapults], and all those who, as they breathe, inhale the powder into their lungs will become asphyxiated." Ever ahead of his time, the inveterate inventor even sketched out a diagram for a simple gas mask.

PLANS OF ATTACK

There are five ways a person can be exposed to poison: ingestion (through the mouth), inhalation (breathed in through the nose or mouth), ocular (in the eyes), dermal (on the skin), and parenteral (from bites or stings).

POISON! (PART II)

(Do not read this until you have read the previous page!)

1. Arsenic is a green powder.

    ☐ **TRUE**   ☐ **FALSE**

2. Parenteral exposure means that poison seeped through the skin.

    ☐ **TRUE**   ☐ **FALSE**

3. The berries of nightshade are poisonous, but not the leaves.

    ☐ **TRUE**   ☐ **FALSE**

4. Socrates was killed by hemlock.

    ☐ **TRUE**   ☐ **FALSE**

5. Wolfsbane does not work immediately.

    ☐ **TRUE**   ☐ **FALSE**

Answers on page 177.

QUICK CRIME QUIZ

How much do you know about the history of crime scene investigation? Answer the following questions.

1. The first fingerprint classification system was created by a police officer working in this country.

☐ **UNITED STATES**

☐ **GREAT BRITAIN**

☐ **ARGENTINA**

2. Do identical twins have identical fingerprints?

☐ **YES** ☐ **NO**

3. Can someone be born without fingerprints?

☐ **YES** ☐ **NO**

4. Can you lose or erode fingerprints?

☐ **YES** ☐ **NO**

5. Can you lift fingerprints from fabric?

☐ **EASILY**

☐ **SOMETIMES, BUT IT IS DIFFICULT**

☐ **NEVER**

Answers on page 177.

DETECTIVES

Complete the word search below to reveal a hidden message related to the puzzle's topic. Every word listed below is contained within the group of letters. Words can be found in a straight line horizontally, vertically, or diagonally. They may read either forward or backward. Once you find all the words, you can read the hidden message from the remaining letters, top to bottom, left to right.

BANACEK	JIM ROCKFORD
BARETTA	McGEE (Travis)
BARNABY (Jones)	MILLER (Barney)
CANNON	NANCY DREW
DICK TRACY	QUEEN (Ellery)
FRIDAY (Sgt.)	QUINCY
HAMMER (Mike)	SPADE (Sam)
HARDY BOYS	THE HARTS
HERCULE POIROT	THE SAINT

Leftover letters spell two of the most famous names in detective fiction, and the author who created them. (six words).

_____

_____

_____

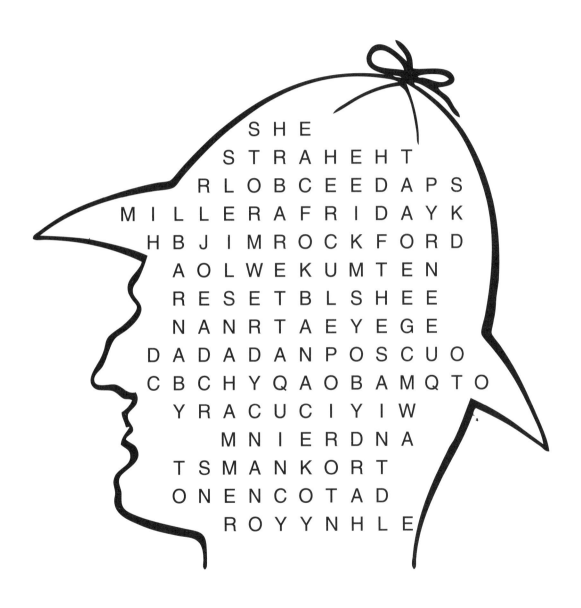

```
        S H E
        S T R A H E H T
        R L O B C E E D A P S
    M I L L E R A F R I D A Y K
    H B J I M R O C K F O R D
    A O L W E K U M T E N
    R E S E T B L S H E E
    N A N R T A E Y E G E
    D A D A D A N P O S C U O
    C B C H Y Q A O B A M Q T O
    Y R A C U C I Y I W
        M N I E R D N A
    T S M A N K O R T
    O N E N C O T A D
    R O Y Y N H L E
```

Answers on page 177.

MECHANIC SHOP

Tune-up your visual skills and spot the 15 differences between the top and the bottom mechanic scenes.

Answers on page 178.

WITNESS STATEMENTS

On Box Street, there are 5 adjacent houses that are identical to each other. You've been asked to interview potential witness Mr. Jones, but without any addresses on the doors you are not sure which house to approach. At the local coffee shop, you ask the waitress for help. She is able to provide the following information:

A. Mr. Jones has 2 neighbors.

B. The house in the middle is occupied by an elderly woman.

C. Mary lives between the elderly woman and a family of 3 children.

D. The 3 children live in House A.

Can you determine which is Mr. Jones's house?

| House A | House B | House C | House D | House E |

Answers on page 178.

SLITHERLINK PATH

Investigators need sharp visual skills and attention to detail. Test your eyes by creating a single continuous path along the dotted lines. The path does not cross itself or touch at any corners. Numbers indicate how many line segments surround each cell. We've filled in some line segments to get you started.

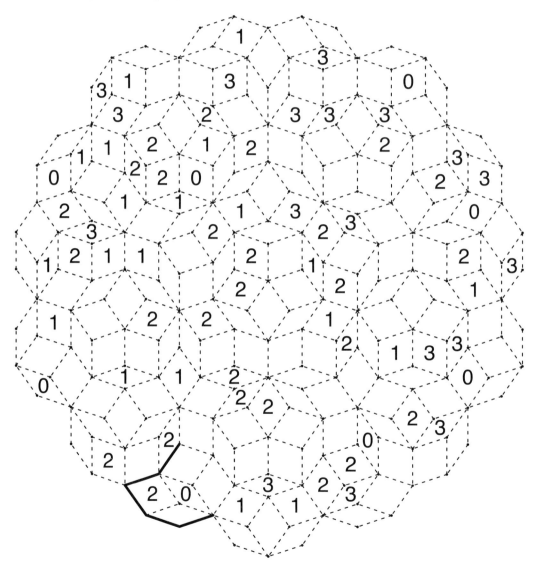

42

Answers on page 178.

KNOT PROBLEM

Which piece of string is knotted, A, B, or C?

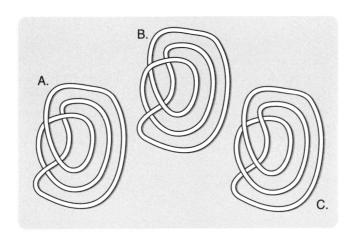

QUIPU

Which of the 3 Quipus (Incan devices for recording information) is identical to the one in the frame? Quipus are considered identical when they can be matched perfectly only by rotating pieces around the knots—they cannot be lifted or turned over. See the example for further clarification.

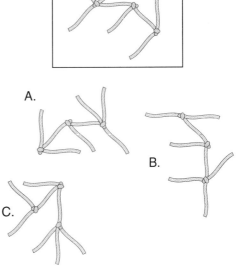

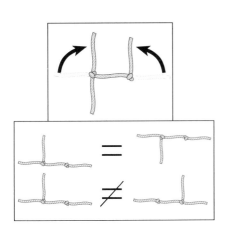

Answers on page 178.

SPY FLY

As an undercover detective tracking down international jewel thieves, your mission is to travel from your headquarters at Seth Castle to your destination at Faro. To disguise your trail, you must stop once—and only once—at each airport. See if you can find the cheapest route for your trip. Less than $280 would make you a Steady Sleuth; less than $270, a Cool Operator; less than $260, a Crafty Agent. If you can make it on $230, then you're a Super Spy!

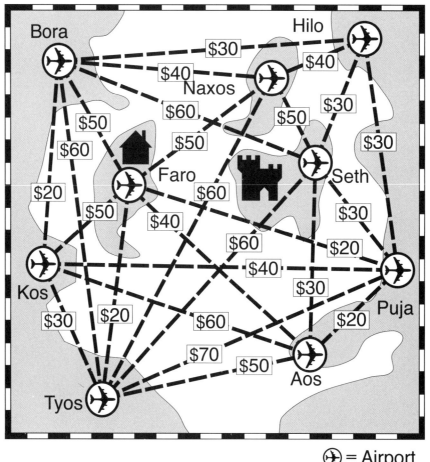

= Airport
= Start
= Finish

44

FIND THE SUSPECT

You're on the track of an escaping criminal, but rain has swept through the entire county, flooding all the bridges indicated by circles. Your job is to travel to each location—A through I, in any order—by restoring only 2 of the bridges.

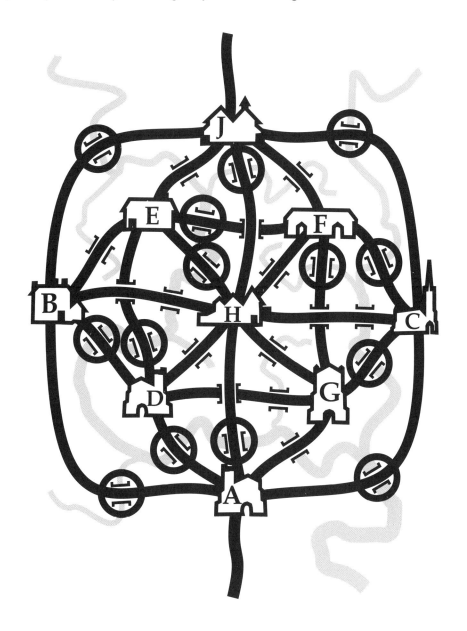

Answers on page 178.

LATIN

Every word listed is contained within the group of letters. Words can be found in a straight line horizontally, vertically, or diagonally. They may be read either forward or backward.

AD INFINITUM	ID EST
AD LIB	IN LOCO PARENTIS
ANTE MERIDIEM	NON SEQUITUR
CIRCA	NOTA BENE
DE FACTO	OP. CIT.
DE JURE	PER ANNUM
DEO GRATIAS	PER DIEM
DEO VOLENTE	PER SE
ET ALIA	PERCENT
ET CETERA	POST MERIDIEM
EX LIBRIS	POST SCRIPTUM
EXAMPLI GRATIA	PRO TEMPORE
IBIDEM	VERSUS

```
L A T I D E O G R A T I A S N
I S P O S T M E R I D I E M U
T S E D I E N E B A T O N U S
P E R D T B I L D A O N T T A
E D C O N M P B R I C S T P D
R E E O E E E G N E B R S I I
A J N F R T I C P O B I I R N
N U T D A L C E C A U S E C F
N R I L P C V E R S U S X S I
U E I M O E T I T T R I L T N
M A A S C A D O E E A D I S I
L X P R O T E M P O R E B O T
E T N E L O V O E D A A R P U
N G U A N T E M E R I D I E M
A R U T I U Q E S N O N S G E
```

47

Answers on page 179.

FINGERPRINT MATCH

Which fingerprint matches the one in the box?

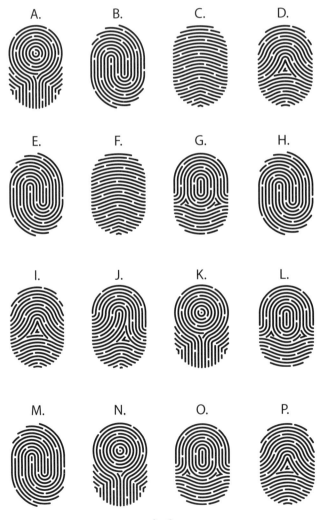

A. B. C. D.

E. F. G. H.

I. J. K. L.

M. N. O. P.

Answers on page 179.

WHAT DO YOU SEE? (PART I)

Study this picture of the crime scene for 1 minute, then turn the page.

WHAT DO YOU SEE? (PART II)

(Do not read this until you have read the previous page!) Which image exactly matches the crime scene?

1.

2.

3.

4.

Answers on page 179.

HIGH FIVES

An investigation at a high school has turned up five names of students who might have been witnesses to a crime. The High Fives school has made a list of these 5 students and each student's subject of study and intended university. Unfortunately, someone has mixed up the details, and although each item is in the correct column, only one item in each column is correctly positioned. The following facts are true about the correct order:

1. Harvard is one place below Harris and one place above economics.
2. Physics is somewhere below Daisy.
3. Arnold is two places above Ink.
4. Philosophy is somewhere above Fate.
5. Yale is one place below physics and one place above Ellen.
6. Daisy is going to MIT.

Can you find the correct name, surname, subject, and university for each position?

	Name	Surname	Subject	University
1	Arnold	Fate	history	Princeton
2	Ben	Gopher	mathematics	Harvard
3	Cathy	Harris	physics	Yale
4	Daisy	Ink	economics	MIT
5	Ellen	Jelly	philosophy	Caltech

Answers on page 179.

DRESSING ROOM

Take a look around this post-game scene. There are 15 differences. Can you find them all?

Answers on page 179.

GAME BOARD (PART I)

Study this game board for one minute, particularly the shapes and their placement. After one minute, turn the page for a memory challenge.

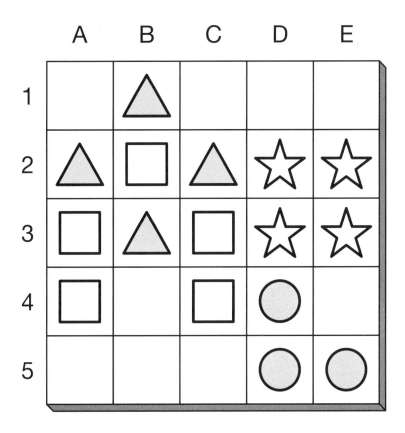

GAME BOARD (PART II)

Do not read this until you've read the previous page!

Duplicate the board as seen on the previous page.

	A	B	C	D	E
1					
2					
3					
4					
5					

Answers on page 179.

WORD TRIO

Fill in each empty box with a different letter so a trio of related words is formed. Hint: these would be good characteristics for a crime scene investigator.

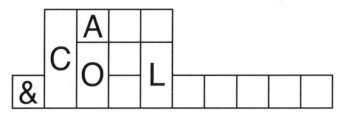

WORD TRIO

Fill in each empty box with a different letter so a trio of related words is formed. Hint: every investigator needs to do this.

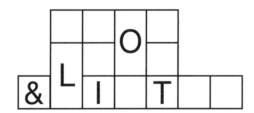

Answers on page 180.

ACROSTIC

Solve the clues below, and then place the letters in their corresponding spots in the grid to reveal a quote by Thomas Carlyle. The letter in the upper-right corner of each grid square refers to the clue the letter comes from. A black square indicates the end of a word.

A.   Shoulder covering

___ ___ ___ ___ ___
49 15 58 68 11

B.   Not hindered or held back

___ ___ ___ ___ ___ ___ ___ ___ ___ ___ ___ ___
7   51 67 25 60 40 1   37 54 70 18 72

C.   Paper bundle

___ ___ ___ ___ ___
39 66 45 2   12

D.   In a cryptic manner

___ ___ ___ ___ ___ ___ ___ ___ ___ ___ ___ ___
21 31 19 27 29 46 48 16 33 56 71 5

E.   Desert danger

___ ___ ___ ___ ___ ___ ___ ___ ___ ___ ___
8   13 43 20 62 42 59 17 24 3   47

F. Allegiance affirmations

— — — — —
50 22 65 28 9

G. Newlyweds, often

— — — — — — — — — — — —
44 32 14 4 36 34 6 69 23 10 57 55

H. "Fight or Flight" chemical

— — — — — — — — — —
61 26 41 38 30 35 53 63 64 52

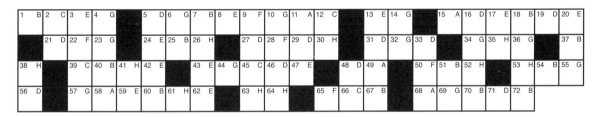

1 B	2 C	3 E	4 G		5 D	6 G	7 B	8 E	9 F	10 G	11 A	12 C		13 E	14 G		15 A	16 D	17 E	18 B	19 D	20 E
	21 D	22 F	23 G		24 E	25 B	26 H		27 D	28 F	29 D	30 H		31 D	32 G	33 D		34 G	35 H	36 G		37 B
38 H		39 C	40 B	41 H	42 E		43 E	44 G	45 C	46 D	47 E		48 D	49 A		50 F	51 B	52 H		53 H	54 B	55 G
56 D		57 G	58 A	59 E	60 B	61 H	62 E		63 H	64 H		65 F	66 C	67 B		68 A	69 G	70 B	71 D	72 B

Answers on page 179.

CRACK THE CODE

Which 2 figures come next in the above sequence?

♣ & ◀ Ω Π Ξ ✝ @ ♣ & ◀ Ω
Π Ξ ✝ @ ♣ & ◀ Ω Π Ξ ✝ @

A. Ω Π   B. ♣ &   C. ♣ ✝   D. ♣ &   E. & ♣

CRACK THE CODE

You've found a series of words. The word that completes the sequence is the criminal's password. What word completes the sequence?

HOTHEAD, SCOLDED, ROMANCE, ABANDON, BATHERS, _____

PLATEAU, ROSEATE, FANTASY, STRETCH, PATTERN

Answers on page 180.

RIDDLE

"Work this one out," said Alice to her work colleague. "I drive from my home to the office every morning. At the back of my house is a short, fairly narrow drive-way approximately 300 yards long. I drive my car down this driveway in a westerly direction, yet when I stop the car at the end of the driveway it is facing east."

"Does the driveway go round in a circle?" asked her colleague.

"No," replied Alice, "it is absolutely straight."

What is the explanation?

WORD LADDER

Change just one letter on each line to go from the top word to the bottom word. Do not change the order of the letters. You must have a common English word at each step.

PASS

_____

_____

_____

WORD

Answers on page 180.

INVESTIGATOR'S KIT

Every word listed is contained within the group of letters. Words can be found in a straight line horizontally, vertically, or diagonally. They may be read either forward or backward.

AUDIO RECORDER

BARRICADE TAPE

BINDLE PAPER

BIOHAZARD BAGS

BOOTIES

CAMERA

CASTING MATERIALS

CHALK

CONSENT TO SEARCH FORMS

FLARES

FLASHLIGHT

GLOVES

LATENT PRINT KIT

MEASURING TAPE

NOTEBOOK

PAPER BAGS

PLASTIC BAGGIES

RULER

SPRAY PAINT

TWEEZERS

```
E  S  S  T  P  F  H  A  P  A  P  E  R  B  A  G  S
P  Y  L  H  S  G  V  Y  K  M  L  R  M  B  C  S  M
A  V  A  G  T  E  C  B  I  O  E  O  S  C  E  G  R
T  A  I  I  I  G  R  X  R  E  A  T  V  P  S  A  O
G  C  R  L  K  O  L  A  H  K  S  N  U  L  V  B  F
N  B  E  H  T  R  O  O  L  I  R  I  B  A  G  D  H
I  E  T  S  N  S  N  B  G  F  E  A  A  S  J  R  C
R  K  A  A  I  E  L  R  B  P  Z  P  R  T  I  A  R
U  L  M  L  R  I  K  U  P  I  E  Y  R  I  K  Z  A
S  A  G  F  P  T  E  L  S  Z  E  A  I  C  B  A  E
A  H  N  C  T  O  C  E  B  J  W  R  C  B  I  H  S
E  C  I  A  N  O  H  R  N  G  T  P  A  A  N  O  O
M  G  T  M  E  B  G  L  O  V  E  S  D  G  D  I  T
F  A  S  E  T  G  T  A  T  J  I  Q  E  G  L  B  T
S  G  A  R  A  V  L  R  E  G  P  R  T  I  E  V  N
S  X  C  A  L  R  L  Q  B  A  X  Z  A  E  P  Z  E
R  T  Y  V  K  H  F  T  O  T  M  B  P  S  A  J  S
A  G  E  B  V  T  I  S  O  U  U  K  E  B  P  W  N
G  I  C  M  V  D  H  E  K  G  K  H  U  J  E  E  O
R  E  D  R  O  C  E  R  O  I  D  U  A  P  R  A  C
```

Answers on page 180.

HOT UNDER THE COLLAR

Cryptograms are messages in substitution code. Break the code to read the message. For example, THE SMART CAT might become FVO QWGDF JGF if **F** is substituted for **T,** **V** for **H, O** for **E,** and so on.

EPIB LQL BPM IZAWVQAB AIG BW PQA AEMMBPMIZB?
K'UWV, JIJG, TQOPB UG NQZM.

SCIENCE WINS!

The words SCIENCE OVER FIEND are an anagram for this two-word phrase related to crime scene investigation. What is it?

_____ _____

MOTEL HIDEOUT

A thief hides out in one of the 45 motel rooms listed in the chart below. The motel's in-house detective received a sheet of four clues, signed "The Holiday Thief." Using these clues, the detective found the room number within 15 minutes—but by that time, the thief had fled. Can you find the thief's motel room quicker?

1. The sum of the digits is greater than 7.
2. The second digit is more than double the first digit.
3. The first digit is divisible by 2.
4. The second digit is divisible by 4.

51	52	53	54	55	56	57	58	59
41	42	43	44	45	46	47	48	49
31	32	33	34	35	36	37	38	39
21	22	23	24	25	26	27	28	29
11	12	13	14	15	16	17	18	19

Answers on page 180.

THE BODY FARM (PART I)

When will an employee not be reprimanded for laying down on the job? When that worker is a Body Farm recruit. Hundreds of rotting corpses get away with such shenanigans every day at the University of Tennessee's "Body Farm," and they have yet to be written up for it. In fact, they are praised for their profound contributions to science. Read the following information, then turn to page 66.

Forensic anthropologist William M. Bass had a dream. As an expert in the field of human decomposition, he couldn't fathom why a facility devoted to this under-studied process didn't exist. So, in 1972, working in conjunction with the University of Tennessee, he founded the Body Farm or, more specifically, the University of Tennessee Forensic Anthropology Facility.

If you're going to start a body farm, it doesn't take a forensic anthropologist to realize that there might be a problem in obtaining bodies. One way is to use bodies that have been donated for medical studies. Another focuses on cadavers that rot away each year at medical examiners offices, with nary a soul to claim them. Enter Bass and his associates.

Just outside of Knoxville, the eerie three-acre wooded plot that Bass claimed for his scientific studies—which is surrounded by a razor wire fence (lest the dead bodies try to escape)—is where an unspecified number of cadavers in various states of decomposition are kept. While some hang out completely in the open, others spend their time in shallow graves or entombed in vaults. Others dip their toes and other body parts in ponds. And a few spend eternity inside sealed car trunks.

So why is this done? What can be learned from observing human flesh and bone decay in the hot Tennessee sun? Plenty, according to scientists and members of the media who have studied the Body Farm. "Nearly everything known about the science of human decomposition comes from one place—forensic anthropologist William Bass' Body Farm," declared CNN in high praise of the facility. The bodies are strewn in different positions and under varying circumstances for reasons far from happenstance. Each cadaver will display differing reactions to decomposition, insect and wildlife interference, and the elements. These invaluable indicators can help investigators zero-in on the cause and time of death in current and future criminal cases.

Bass himself claims that knowledge gleaned from Body Farm studies has proven especially helpful to murder investigations. "People will have alibis for certain time periods, and if you can determine death happened at another time, it makes a difference in the court case," said Bass. Even the prestigious FBI uses the Body Farm as a real-world simulator to help train its agents. Every February, representatives visit the site to dig for bodies that farm hands have prepared as simulated crime scenes. "We have five of them down there for them," explains Bass. "They excavate the burials and look for evidence that we put there."

Although many other proposed farms never got off the ground due to community protest, since the inception of Bass's original Body Farm, other facilities have been established, including one at Western Carolina University. Ideally, Bass would like to see body farms all over the nation. Since decaying bodies react differently depending on their climate and surroundings, says Bass, "It's important to gather information from other research facilities across the United States."

Such is life down on the Body Farm.

THE BODY FARM (PART II)

(Do not read this until you have read the previous page!)

1. The Body Farm is the only facility of its kind in the United States.

☐ **TRUE**   ☐ **FALSE**

2. One thing studied at the Body Farm is how insects can affect decomposition of cadavers.

☐ **TRUE**   ☐ **FALSE**

3. The Body Farm is a training site for investigators.

☐ **TRUE**   ☐ **FALSE**

4. Climate can greatly affect decomposition rates.

☐ **TRUE**   ☐ **FALSE**

5. The Body Farm was founded in 1942.

☐ **TRUE**   ☐ **FALSE**

Answers on page 180.

WHAT DO YOU SEE? (PART I)

Study this picture of the crime scene for 1 minute, then turn the page.

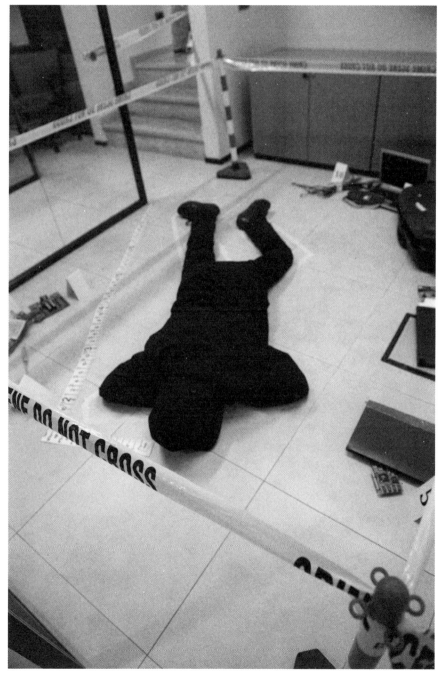

WHAT DO YOU SEE (PART II)

(Do not read this until you have read the previous page!)

Which image exactly matches the crime scene?

1.

2.

3.

4.

68

Answers on page 180.

QUICK CRIME QUIZ

1. A Chinese book from the 13th century, Hsi DuanYu (the Washing Away of Wrongs) described this:

☐ **HOW TO TELL DROWNING FROM STRANGULATION**

☐ **HOW TO TELL DROWNING FROM NATURAL DEATH**

☐ **HOW TO TELL HEART ATTACK FROM STRANGULATION**

2. The first instance of bullet comparison being used to solve a murder occurred in this century:

☐ **1600s** ☐ **1700s** ☐ **1800s** ☐ **1900s**

3. In the U.S., the first use of DNA evidence to solve a crime occurred in this decade.

☐ **1970s** ☐ **1980s** ☐ **1990s**

4. Scientist Karl Landsteiner established that there were different blood types in this decade.

☐ **1830s** ☐ **1900s** ☐ **1970s**

5. The FBI was founded in this year.

☐ **1888s** ☐ **1908s** ☐ **1932s**

Answers on page 181.

ALL SECRET PLOTS LEAVE CLUES

Change just one letter on each line to go from the top word to the bottom word. Do not change the order of the letters. You must have a common English word at each step.

PLOTS

_____

_____

_____

_____

_____

CLUES

A CASE OF ARSON

Change just one letter on each line to go from the top word to the bottom word. Do not change the order of the letters. You must have a common English word at each step.

FIRE

_____

_____

_____

_____

CASE

Answers on page 181.

IDENTITY PARADE

Oops! Four mugshots accidentally got sent through the shredder, and Officer Wallers is trying to straighten them out. Currently, only one facial feature in each row is in its correct place. Officer Wallers knows that:

1. C's nose is 1 place to the right of her mouth and 2 places to the right of D's hair.

2. C's eyes are 2 places to the left of her hair.

3. A's eyes are 1 place to the right of B's nose and 1 place to the right of D's mouth.

Can you find the correct hair, eyes, nose, and mouth for each person?

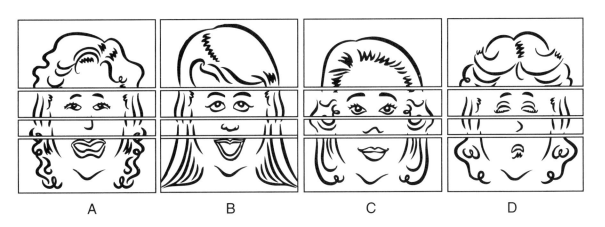

| A | B | C | D |

Answers on page 181.

KNOWNS AND UNKNOWNS (PART 1)

Study the synopsis of the crime, then turn to page 74 to test your knowledge.

Victim:

Priscilla A. Hrupington

Cause of death:

Stabbed by a set of gardening shears.

Approximate time of death:

between 10 PM on Friday evening and 1 AM on Saturday morning.

Location:

Found dead in hotel room 218 by housekeeping at ~8:30 AM, Saturday, May 21. The hotel was in California; the victim lived in Ohio. The hotel was hosting a convention at the time, the annual convention for the organization Growers of Roses & Orchids in Extreme Environments (GOREE). Hrupington was a registered member of the convention, and her program, name badge, and materials were found in her room. The program showed that on Friday afternoon during the 2 PM-2:50 time slot, she was scheduled to be part of a panel on mulch, and her fellow panelists, when interviewed, said that it had gone smoothly and without incident.

Details:

Dolores Simonova, the hotel housekeeper, knocked on the door and did not receive a response. The placard on the door read, "Housekeeping please." Simonova opened the door using her master key card. The chain was not on, nor was the deadbolt in place. Simonova entered the room and immediately saw Hrupington. She says that she gave "a short scream" but no one came in response. She backed out of the room and blocked the entryway with her cart, then immediately alerted the hotel's manager through walkie-talkie. The hotel's manager called 911 (call logged 8:42 AM). Simonova did not remember seeing Hrupington at any point previously. She had cleaned the room the previous day and not encountered her then.

The victim was lying face up on the bed, on top of the bedspread. She was dressed in blouse, pants, underwear, and socks. A blazer had been left on a nearby chair. A watch, brooch, and bracelet were found on the end table by the bed. There were no signs of struggle.

Hrupington's purse had been left at the scene. Inside were a driver's license and credit cards. There was an ATM receipt from Wednesday the 18th indicating that Hrupington had withdrawn $80, but no cash was found. A smartphone was found in the purse.

No laptop was found, although Hrupington's roommate (Patricia E. Flugelflugh) stated that she had one. Flugelflugh said that it was not at the apartment she shared with the victim (search of shared apartment confirms). She stated that Hrupington sometimes brought it with her on travel and sometimes did not. Flugelflugh also said the victim might have left it at her boyfriend's residence, as she often spent the time there, did work when she did so, and left the laptop there for several days.

The victim's boyfriend of 6 months (Kenneth E. Fogletrutt) also attested that the victim had owned a laptop. He said that the victim had been wavering about whether to bring it and may have decided against it, but it was not at his apartment. He also implied that the reason Hrupington often left it at his apartment was that the victim's roommate was untrustworthy and that Hrupington was planning on moving out when the lease was up. Flugelflugh denied this, saying that Fogletrutt was "shady in small ways," that he took advantage of Hrupington's trusting nature by often borrowing money from her, and that if Hrupington was planning on moving out it was "news to her."

Both agreed that the gardening shears were not the victim's, as they did not recognize in. In addition, the victim flew and would not have been able to take anything of the sort through airport security.

KNOWNS AND UNKNOWNS (PART II)

(Do not read this until you have read the previous page!)

1. The murderer stole Hrupington's laptop.

☐ TRUE   ☐ POSSIBLY TRUE   ☐ FALSE

2. A local thief broke in to Hrupington's room to steal valuables and was interrupted, leading to the murder.

☐ SEEMS LIKELY   ☐ SEEMS UNLIKELY

3. The murderer stole $80 cash from the scene of the crime.

☐ TRUE   ☐ POSSIBLY TRUE   ☐ FALSE

4. The murderer brought the gardening shears to the scene of the crime.

☐ SEEMS LIKELY   ☐ SEEMS UNLIKELY

5. The victim was found on Saturday morning but was killed on Friday morning.

☐ TRUE   ☐ POSSIBLY TRUE   ☐ FALSE

Answers on page 181.

FINGERPRINT MATCH

There are eight sets of fingerprints. Find each match.

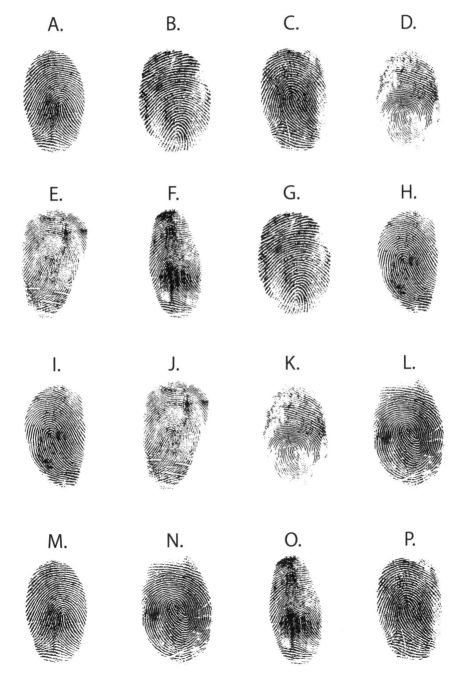

A. B. C. D.

E. F. G. H.

I. J. K. L.

M. N. O. P.

Answers on page 181.

WITNESS STATEMENTS (PART I)

Other convention participants and hotel dwellers were interviewed to trace Hrupington's movements during the GOREE conference (see pages 72-73). They are presented below in the order collected. Read and then turn to page 78.

Rebecca Thrush (front desk clerk at hotel): Processed Hrupington's check-in on Thursday evening as part of a rush of travelers who came in around 8 PM from an airport shuttle that runs every half-hour. Computer records show Hrupington's reservation as being processed at 8:13 PM. Thrush's interaction with Hrupington was neutral and standard. Thrush did not remember if Hrupington had been interacting with other people in the check-in line. As per hotel policy, she did not announce Hrupington's room number aloud, but wrote in on the keycard slip that she handed over to Hrupington.

Kenneth Smith (business traveler, room 216): Smith checked in on Friday at approximately 11 AM (hotel records confirm). He was not attending the convention, but traveling for business. Smith did not remember seeing Hrupington at any point. On Friday evening, Smith returned to his room after a business dinner at approximately 9 PM. At some point later than that, he heard people walking down the hall outside his room and a female voice said, "Bye, Prissy!" before hearing sounds like someone entering the room next to his. Shortly thereafter, the television turned on. He did not hear voices but didn't rule out a guest. Could have been anytime between 9:30 and 11 PM, when Smith went to bed. He did not hear any unusual sounds during the night, but wears earplugs while on business trips.

Freesia Jones (convention goer, room 220): Knew the victim. She and Hrupington had met at previous yearly conventions and maintained an occasional e-mail correspondence between times, focused on plant care. She saw Hrupington leave her hotel room on Friday morning around 9 AM as they both headed to the morning panels. They made plans to attend a 2 PM panel on Saturday together and go for a coffee afterwards to catch up. (Hrupington's phone confirms the appointment.) Jones did not attend the victim's mulch panel at 2 PM as she was manning a flower booth from 1-3 Friday. She knocked on Hrupington's hotel door at 7 PM to see if she wanted to go to dinner with Freesia and two other convention attendees, but there was no response. Jones returned to her hotel room at about

11:30 PM. She did not hear remember hearing a TV in the other room at that time. She went to bed around midnight, and thought she might have heard someone walk down the hallway and enter the victim's room, or another room nearby, not long afterward, rousing her briefly from a light sleep. She woke up at 7 AM and did not hear any noises from the victim's room.

Wendall Waxman (convention goer, moderator of Friday's mulch panel, room 201): Had corresponded with Hrupington via e-mail after the panel assignments were announced in January and had "seen her in passing before," but had first spoken to her in person at the panel itself. Described her as "polite, knowledgeable, calm," did not speak much of her personal life. Said the panel was successful and that there were no conflicts between panelists. Nothing inflammatory/controversial was said and the response from the audience was good. Had not seen Hrupington afterwards, but thought it possible that they could have attended some of the same larger panels. Had not seen Hrupington on their shared floor.

Rebecca Podunski (convention goer, panelist alongside Hrupington, room 308): Had met Hrupington before at previous conventions; did not correspond between times. Described her as doing "solid but not groundbreaking work." Said the panel was for her taste a bit staid, but Waxman, Hrupington, and most of the audience seemed to want it that way. Said victim was at 4 PM panel on rose hybrids that was "deathly boring" and spent much of her time on her smartphone but then asked question at the end.

Heather White (waitstaff, hotel restaurant and bar): White was on duty both Thursday night 6-11 PM and Friday night 6-midnight. Victim came to hotel bar on Thursday night at 10 PM, alone, and sat in 2-seat table. Had a drink or two, a few small tapas plates (hotel credit card receipts confirm). Chatted briefly with other people who would stop at her table (White identified one of them as Waxman.) On Friday, came to restaurant with group ~6:30 PM. Group of four, two women, two men. Paid in pooled cash. White said conversation seemed friendly, conversational. Group closed out tab, paying in cash, and left together around 8:00.

WITNESS STATEMENTS (PART II)

(Do not read this until you have read the previous page!)

Put together a timeline of the victim's final days by matching a time on the left to an event on the right:

Thursday, 8 PM	Freesia Jones sees Hrupington outside their rooms
Thursday, 10 PM	
	Hrupington attends dinner at hotel restaurant
Friday, 9 AM	
	Hrupington moderates mulch panel Hrupington checks into hotel
Friday, 2 PM	
Friday, 4 PM	Hrupington visits hotel bar
Friday, 6:30 PM	Hrupington leaves restaurant
Friday, 8 PM	Hrupington attends rose panel
Friday, post-9 PM	Smith hears movement in room next to his (Hrupington's)

Bonus: Do you spot a discrepancy in any of the witness statements?

Answers on page 181.

EAVESDROPPING LOGIC

Two women walk into your shop discussing someone standing just outside. "She can't hear a thing from here," mutters the first one. "I don't know, she's looking at us very strangely," replies the second. "Serves her right if she hears something she doesn't want to, after what she's done," says the first. "It's not her fault really," says her friend, to which the first woman raises her eyebrows.

Which of the following is the most accurate considering what you have overheard?

A. The woman outside has done something to upset the 2 women in the shop.

B. The woman outside has done something bad.

C. The 2 women inside the shop are fighting over whether to remain friends with the woman outside.

D. The 2 women inside the shop are disagreeing over whether the woman outside is at fault for something.

CRACK THE PASSWORD

You've found a sequence that might be the criminal's password. Can you complete this sequence and crack the password?

T G S ___ E

Answers on page 181.

MIXED-UP MARRIAGES

On Saturday, a crime was committed at a local church. 6 marriages were due to be performed throughout the day, and police are trying to track down the order. However, the details of the brides and grooms have been inadvertently mixed up in the planner. Although each name is in the correct column, only one name in each column is correctly positioned. The following facts are certain about the correct order:

1. Yates is two places below Goliath.

2. Colin is one place below Idi.

3. Fred is three places below Nina, who is two above Underwood.

4. Vitori is somewhere below Olive, who is somewhere below Kite.

5. James is one place above Pauline, who is two places above Doug.

6. Rosie is one place above Abe, who is one above Stephens.

Can you give the first and last names of the groom and bride for each position?

	Groom 1st	Groom 2nd	Bride 1st	Bride 2nd
1	Abe	Goliath	Minnie	Stephens
2	Bill	Holderness	Nina	Tallis
3	Colin	Idi	Olive	Underwood
4	Doug	James	Pauline	Vitori
5	Eddie	Kite	Alice	Wells
6	Fred	Leonard	Rosie	Yates

Answers on page 181.

TAILGATE PARTY

These fans are cooking up some fun before the game! Find 10 things that are different between the 2 pictures.

81

Answers on page 182.

WITNESS STATEMENTS

On Box Street, there are 5 adjacent houses that are identical to each other. You've been asked to visit Mr. Linus and gather his witness statemnent, but without any addresses on the doors you are not sure which house to approach. At the local coffee shop, you ask the waitress for help. She is able to provide the following information:

A. Mr. Linus does not like dogs.

B. The dog living next door to Mr. Linus often tunnels under his other neighbor's fence to chase their cat.

C. There are no animals at House B.

D. House A owns a cat.

E. House C owns a cat.

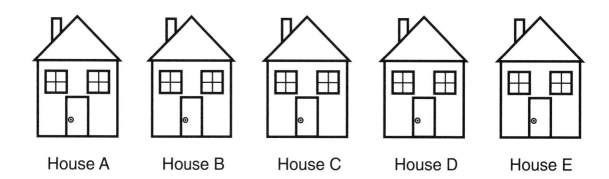

| House A | House B | House C | House D | House E |

MOTEL HIDEOUT

A thief hides out in one of the 45 motel rooms listed in the chart below. The motel's in-house detective received a sheet of four clues, signed "The Holiday Thief." Using these clues, the detective found the room number within 15 minutes—but by that time, the thief had fled. Can you find the thief's motel room quicker?

1. The first digit and the second digit are one digit apart (e.g, 34, 56).

2. The sum of the digits is five or greater.

3. It is divisible by 3.

4. It is less than seven squared.

51	52	53	54	55	56	57	58	59
41	42	43	44	45	46	47	48	49
31	32	33	34	35	36	37	38	39
21	22	23	24	25	26	27	28	29
11	12	13	14	15	16	17	18	19

Answers on page 182.

MASTER OF SUSPENSE

ACROSS

1. Trumpet, for one
5. Bronze, e.g.
10. First: abbr.
14. Slurpee rival
15. Covent Garden architect Jones
16. Detective Wolfe
17. 1938 thriller starring Margaret Lockwood
20. Square of turf
21. Dies _____ (Latin hymn)
22. Metamorphic rock
23. CBS forensics drama
24. State sch. in Tucson
25. 1945 Ingrid Bergman/Gregory Peck thriller
30. The m in E=mc
34. Contend
35. Lost traction
36. All _____ up (agitated)
37. Tiresome one
38. Concert pianist André
39. A few bucks?
40. Nice summer
41. Beanstalk giant, e.g.
42. Sporty car
43. College mil. offering
45. 1954 James Stewart/Grace Kelly thriller
47. Bookie's numbers
49. Suffix with sulf-
50. Like some escapes
53. Shake _____
55. Duffel
58. 1947 courtroom drama starring Gregory Peck
61. Afflictions
62. Love, Italian-style
63. Sports cable channel
64. Little fella
65. Beeper
66. For fear that

DOWN

1. Top 40 songs
2. Eight, in Ecuador
3. Singer Lou
4. "_____ Blu, Dipinto Di Blu"
5. Central vein of a leaf
6. One-named Irish singer
7. Seedy bar
8. Khan title
9. Unfavorable probability
10. Pants measurement
11. Classic soft drink
12. Makes mad
13. Deep-six
18. Wedding walkway
19. Army div.
23. These very words
24. Person who brings others together
25. Fencing sword
26. Type starter
27. Everglades wader
28. Oil-rich Indians
29. To-the-max prefix
31. Out in front
32. Take care of
33. "That's the last _____!"
38. Text-editing feature
39. Take a meal
42. Winged nuisance
44. Body of mysteries
46. Frankfurter
48. Dennis Quaid movie
50. Cereal box stat
51. Sailor's call
52. Smell to high heaven
53. Work like _____
54. Milano moola, once
55. Foundation

56. Nile reptiles
57. Lady's man
59. Doc bloc
60. Animation frame

Answers on page 182.

IDENTITY PARADE

Oops! Four mugshots accidentally got sent through the shredder, and Officer Cuse is trying to straighten them out. Currently, only one facial feature in each row is in its correct place. Officer Cuse knows that:

1. C's eyes are one place to the right of his hair and 2 places to the right of D's nose.

2. A's mouth is one place ot the right of B's eyes and one place to the left of D's hair.

3. C's mouth is 2 places to the left of his nose.

4. B's hair is one place to the right of C's eyes.

Can you find the correct hair, eyes, nose, and mouth for each person?

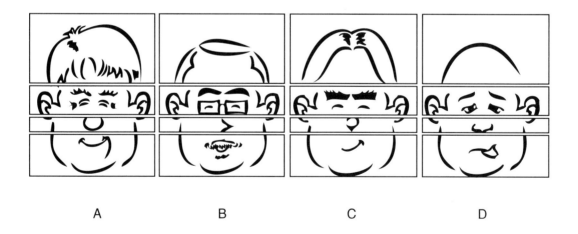

A   B   C   D

Answers on page 182.

WHERE DOES ARSON FIT?

To complete this puzzle, place the given letters and words into the shapes in this grid. Words and letters will run across, down, and wrap around each shape. When the grid is filled, each row will contain one of the following words: bolts, fools, liars, spoon, stamp, tawas

1. O, S
2. AT, SS
3. OWL
4. FOOT, LAMP, SLIP, STAB
5. ARSON

Answers on page 182.

FIND THE SUSPECT

You're on the trail of a suspect, but rain has swept through the entire county, flooding all the bridges indicated by circles. Your job is to travel to each location—A through I, in any order—by restoring only 2 of the bridges.

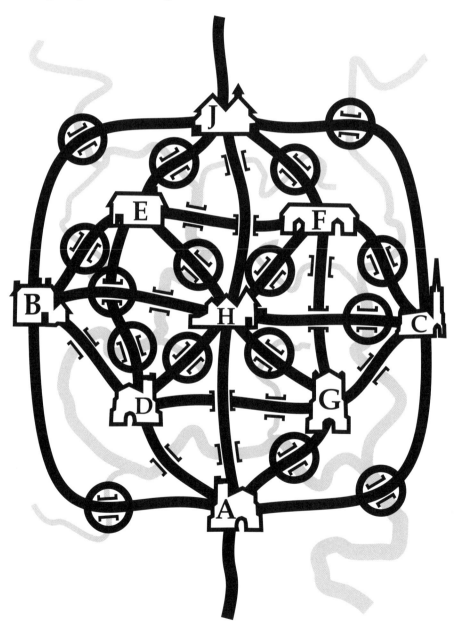

Answers on page 182.

CHEMICAL REACTION

A certain chemical compound is formed by mixing 2 different chemicals. The first chemical is worth $90 per ounce; the second is worth $40 per ounce. The blend of chemicals is valued at $70 per ounce. How many ounces of the $90 chemical are needed to make 40 ounces of the blend?

A. 8

B. 16

C. 24

D. 30

NUMBER SEQUENCE

What number comes next?

2 5 14 41 122 365 ?

Answers on page 183.

SHROUDED SUMMARY

Hidden in the word search is a summary of a well-known novel. The words you need to find are listed below in alphabetical order; in the word search they are presented in an order that makes more sense. Words can be found in straight line horizontally, vertically, or diagonally. As a bonus, can you name the novel and its author?

BECOMES

BLACKMAIL

BOTH

CASE

DAUGHTERS

DETECTIVE

DYING

ENTWINED

FOR

HIRES

INVOLVING

SCANDALS

TYCOON

WHICH

WITH

Novel and author:

_____

_____

```
S T H P Y J Q A B O U L A
D Y I N G F L U S F L I N
A C R K B L C M I L D U H
T O E V I T C E T E D E R
S O S F R T C N O Y F B E
C N M E S D E T T V O E C
H I R D F S W E S B R W H
C H B O H T H C L D Y H K
I G N I V O I A L V N G I
W I H Y T W C S C A E S E
N T W N D K H E I E S C A
N D S E M O C E B A L S B
L A C A N K M D A F O T Y
B C I D E T H I W I H B O
T L H D Y G W I T H I V O
L V I G W T H I I C S Q P
E W U I M S C A N D A L S
H E I E S C A X V E B K J
A N F R L D H T O B D Q M
B K M L W H T C L L A H D
H I R D F S W E V J U L K
F H I S T W D E I B G C B
M I L D U H N I N M H D S
B C O M L B S T G J T I B
M U S I M P I C E D E R E
S I S T N S E D E L R A C
E O U E R M O U L N S A R
```

91

PICTURE THIS

Place each of the 18 boxes in the 6 by 3 grid below so they form an ice-cool picture. Do this without cutting the page apart: Use only your eyes. Two boxes will remain blank.

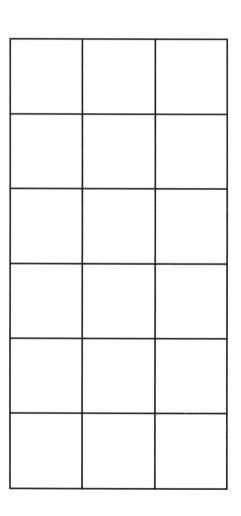

Answers on page 183.

BACK UP YOUR MEMORY (PART 1)

Study these words and illustrations for one minute then turn the page for a memory challenge.

Backache

Backboard

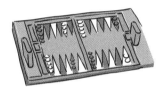

Backgammon

Backpack

Backflip

Backfire

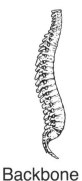

Backbone

BACK UP YOUR MEMORY (PART II)

How many of these did you see on the previous page?

BACKBOARD

BACK TEETH

BACKFIELD

BACKPACK

BACKSEAT

BACKSTITCH

BACKSTOP

BACK FLIP

BACKGAMMON

BACKGROUND

Answers on page 183.

GLOBE QUEST

You're tracking down an interstate criminal, following him around the country. You know he'll visit 9 cities that host his criminal enterprises, and (fortunately for your agency's budget) that he'll try to find the cheapest flights. What route do you anticipate him taking?

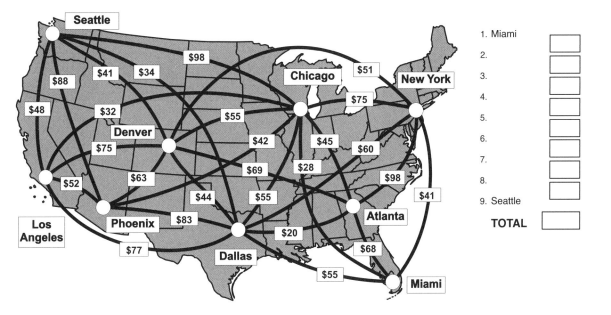

1. Miami

2.

3.

4.

5.

6.

7.

8.

9. Seattle

TOTAL

Answers on page 183.

CRACK THE CODE

The 8 symbols each represent a different number between 1 and 10. The numbers to the right and below the grid show the totals of that row or column. Can you deduce the numerical value of each symbol?

❖	☐	❖	❄	◆	❄	◐	✳	53
☐	●	✳	◆	❄	◐	✳	✳	44
◐	✳	◐	●	◐	◆	☐	◐	38
●	◆	❄	❖	◆	☐	✳	❖	44
☐	●	◐	✳	●	✳	☐	◐	36
✳	◆	✳	❖	❄	◐	✳	✳	50
☐	✳	❖	●	✳	✳	◐	✳	45
❖	☐	❄	◆	❄	●	✳	❖	50
42	28	62	41	50	41	44	52	

Answers on page 183.

SEEN AT THE SCENE (PART 1)

A crime took place in a Christmas-themed store! Study these illustrations for one minute then turn the page for a memory challenge.

Nutcracker

Santa

Reindeer

Elf

Candy cane

Sled

Snowman

Sleigh bell

Santa's sleigh

SEEN AT THE SCENE (PART II)

Do not read this until you have read the previous page!

Circle the words you saw illustrated on the previous page.

SANTA

STOCKING

ANGEL

ELF

SNOWMAN

GLOBE

TOBOGGAN

PICTURE FRAME

REINDEER

SLEIGH BELL

Answers on page 184.

CANDY SHOP

There was a robbery at the candy shop. The store owner is trying to figure out how much was stolen. Before the robbery, four friends came in. The store owner is trying to figure out which of them bought what and how much they spent. Determine the first and last name of each friend, what they purchased, and the amount of money each one spent on candy (possible amounts are $1.00, $1.25, $1.50, and $1.75).

1. Monica didn't buy chocolate. Denise's last name isn't Hall.
2. Anne, who bought gum balls, spent less than the girl whose last name is Smith.
3. Ms. Page didn't buy licorice.
4. Ms. Hall spent 25 cents more than the girl who bought the Swedish fish but 50 cents less than Monica.
5. Sally's last name is Jones but she didn't buy Swedish fish.

First Name	Last Name	Type of Candy	Amount Spent

Answers on page 184.

FORENSIC CAREERS

Every word listed is contained within the group of letters. Words can be found in a straight line horizontally, vertically, or diagonally. They may be read either forward or backward.

ACCOUNTANT

ANTHROPOLOGIST

BALLISTICS EXPERT

BIOLOGIST

BOTANIST

CHEMIST

COMPUTER ANALYST

DENTIST

DNA ANALYST

DOCUMENTS EXAMINER

ENTOMOLOGIST

INVESTIGATOR

LAB TECHNICIAN

MEDICAL EXAMINER

NURSE

ODONTOLOGY

PATHOLOGIST

PSYCHOLOGIST

SCIENCE TECHNICIAN

TOXICOLOGIST

```
Y P W Z B Z P P R D C H E M I S T
G K Q W P A C C O U N T A N T S V
O T J I W U A F F U G T G A I L R
L M E D I C A L E X A M I N E R E
O L A B T E C H N I C I A N T G N
T S I G O L O P O R H T N A U T I
N P D G N M Z V O C O Y E V V J M
O V A U H S O R L B J C U V A K A
D T R D E N T O M O L O G I S T X
O S I N V E S T I G A T O R P J E
E S I G Q F C E S X M U T Z A A S
P S Y C H O L O G I S T B F K W T
R T S I T N E D Q D G L N G U S N
Z T H I L P A T H O L O G I S T E
P K B N U M D N A A N A L Y S T M
T O X I C O L O G I S T B O D N U
T K X R Q U R R I Z Z P H U I W C
T S Y L A N A R E T U P M O C B O
T R E P X E S C I T S I L L A B D
N A I C I N H C E T E C N E I C S
```

Answers on page 184.

CRIME RHYMES

Each clue leads to a 2-word answer that rhymes, such as BIG PIG or STABLE TABLE. The numbers in parentheses after the clue give the number of letters in each word. For example, "cookware taken from the oven (3, 3)" would be "hot pot."

1. Suspect swore he was getting fast food (3, 5): _____

2. Arsonist who hated musical instruments set this (4, 4): _____

3. Murder at the racetrack (12, 4): _____

4. Cantaloupe thief (5, 5): _____

5. Scoff at idea of using this poison (5, 7): _____

6. Provided poison (8, 7): _____

7. Noisy diamond heist (3, 6): _____

8. When the funeral home thought something might be going on (9, 9): _____

PERFECT PAIRS

Use the letter tiles given to complete the word pairs. Each pair of words will be a homonyms of one another.

The ME recorded everything she had _ _ _ _ at the _C_ _ _.

E E E E N N S S

Answers on page 184.

MOTEL HIDEOUT

A thief hides out in one of the 45 motel rooms listed in the chart below. The motel's in-house detective received a sheet of four clues, signed "The Holiday Thief." Using these clues, the detective found the room number within 15 minutes—but by that time, the thief had fled. Can you find the thief's motel room quicker?

1. The first digit is larger than the second.

2. The second digit is not 3 or 4.

3. It is not divisible by 3.

4. It is divisible by 4.

51	52	53	54	55	56	57	58	59
41	42	43	44	45	46	47	48	49
31	32	33	34	35	36	37	38	39
21	22	23	24	25	26	27	28	29
11	12	13	14	15	16	17	18	19

Answers on page 184.

FINGERPRINT MATCH

Find one or more fingerprints that match the one in the box.

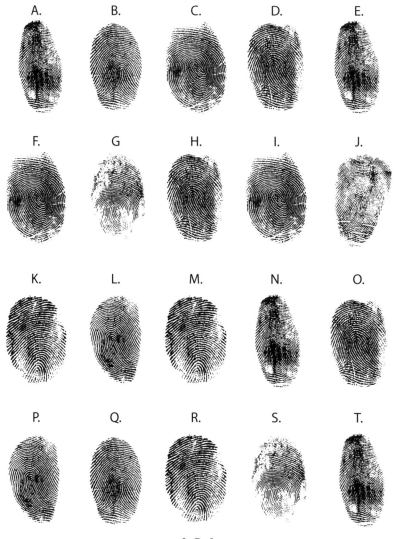

A.   B.   C.   D.   E.

F.   G.   H.   I.   J.

K.   L.   M.   N.   O.

P.   Q.   R.   S.   T.

Answers on page 184.

WHAT DO YOU SEE? (PART 1)

Study this picture of the crime scene for 1 minute, then turn the page.

WHAT DO YOU SEE? (PART II)

(Do not read this until you have read the previous page!)

1. There was a small placard on the floor with a number on it. What was that number?

A. 1

B. 2

C. 3

D. 4

2. How many markers were on the table?

A. 1

B. 2

C. 3

D. 4

3. Was there any writing on any of the papers?

☐ YES   ☐ NO

4. A chair had been overturned.

☐ YES   ☐ NO

Answers on page 184.

EAVESDROPPING LOGIC

You overhear one woman accusing another of listening in on her private conversation with her boyfriend. You only hear a piece of the accused woman's response, which sounds like, "I'm sorry, nobody ould have heard you, but..."

Which of the following words would best fit in the place of "ould", assuming the woman was being genuinely apologetic?

A. "should"

B. "could"

C. "would"

D. All of the above would fit with this assumption

CRACK THE PASSWORD

Can you complete this sequence to crack the criminal's password?

L, L, A T ___ O H

Answers on page 185.

WITNESS STATEMENTS

On Box Street, there are 5 adjacent houses that are identical to each other. You've been asked to visit Mr. Foreman, but without any addresses on the doors, you are not sure which house to approach. At the local coffee shop, you ask the waitress for help. She is able to provide the following information:

1. Two of the 5 houses contain children and adults.

2. Mr. Foreman lives alone.

3. Both houses with children have 2 neighboring properties and are not adjacent to each other.

4. The children often pass through Mrs. Cato's garden to play with each other.

5. The residents of the house located 2 spots to the right of Mrs. Cato's get along well with everyone on the street.

Which house does Mr. Foreman live in?

House A

House B

House C

House D

House E

Answers on page 185.

DIVE RIGHT IN

Find the 10 differences between these swimmer scenes.

109

FIND THE SUSPECT

You're in pursuit of a criminal, but rain has swept through the entire county, flooding all the bridges indicated by circles. Your job is to travel to each location—A through I, in any order—by restoring only 2 of the bridges.

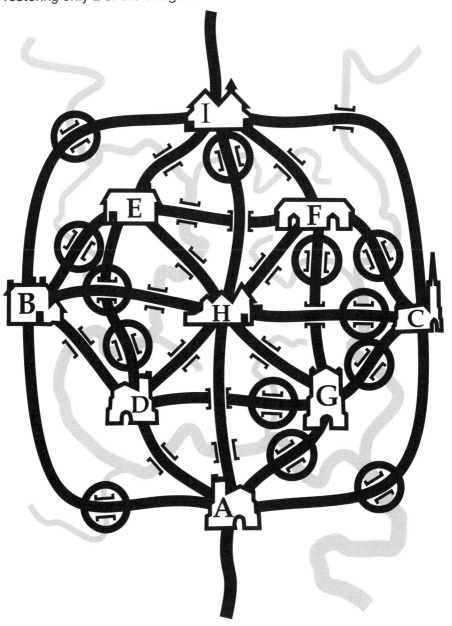

Answers on page 185.

GAME BOARD (PART I)

Study this game board for one minute, particularly the shapes and their placement. Then turn the page for a memory challenge.

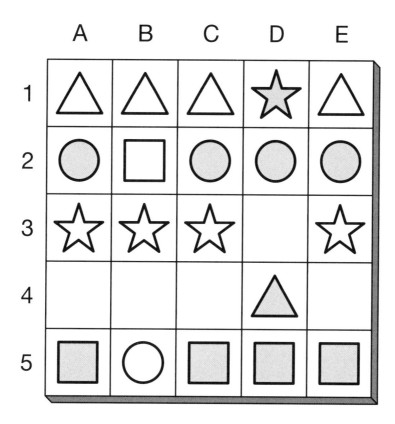

GAME BOARD (PART II)

Do not read this until you have read the previous page!

Duplicate the board as seen on the previous page.

	A	B	C	D	E
1					
2					
3					
4					
5					

Answers on page 185.

KNOT PROBLEM

Which of the 2 rings of string are linked together, A or B?

A.

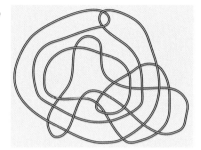

B.

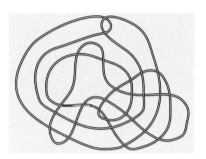

ANAGRAMMAR

One side of the torn parchment from the crime scene shows a word. The other side is meant to contain an anagram of that word that will tell you the password. Trace the lines connecting identical letter to find out what the second word is.

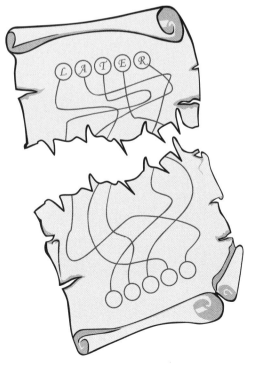

Answers on page 185.

ANAGRAMMAR

One side of the torn parchment from the crime scene shows a word. The other side is meant to contain an anagram of that word that will tell you the password. Trace the lines connecting identical letter to find out what the second word is.

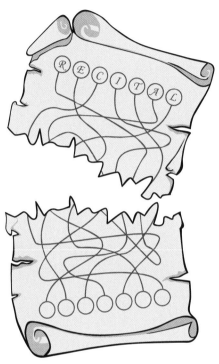

TO THE LETTER

Fill in the blanks with words that are nearly identical to each other. Figure out the first word, then drop one letter to discover the second word. Do not rearrange the letters.

It may be dangerous to _____ a person who snatches your _____.

Answers on page 185.

SEEN AT THE SCENE (PART I)

Which tools were found at the scene of the crime? Study the page for a minute, then turn the page for a memory challenge.

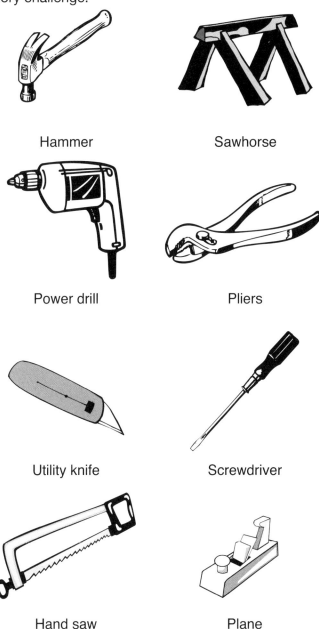

Hammer	Sawhorse
Power drill	Pliers
Utility knife	Screwdriver
Hand saw	Plane

SEEN AT THE SCENE (PART II)

Do not look at this until you have read the previous page!

Check off the tools you saw on the previous page.

CIRCULAR SAW

PLIERS

PIPE WRENCH

LATHE

PLANE

SAWHORSE

LEVEL

RULER

CROWBAR

CHISEL

HAMMER

HAND SAW

UTILITY KNIFE

Answers on page 186.

TO THE LETTER

Fill in the blanks with words that are nearly identical to each other. Figure out the first word, then drop one letter to discover the second word. Do not rearrange the letters.

The man got quite a _____ once faced with

the prospect of getting into a _____.

KNOT PROBLEM

If you pull each end of the strings in figures A, B, and C in the direction of the arrow, which string will not be knotted? For insight into knotted and unknotted string, see the example below. The figure on the left is unknotted; the figure on the right is knotted.

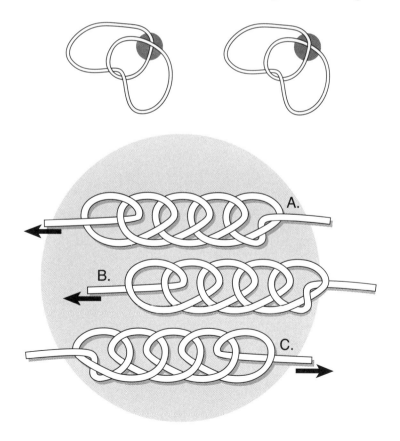

Answers on page 186.

THE RINGMAKER

David Jeffries is a custom ring designer. Every ring he makes is 100 percent unique—no design of his is ever used twice. This week he has 5 customers coming to pick up their rings, each of which has a different type of metal band (platinum, silver, titanium, etc.) and a different type of precious stone (amethyst, diamond, emerald, etc.). Each customer has received a message telling them to come into the store on a particular day to pick up their ring. Using only the clues and chart below, determine the type of metal and precious stone used in each customer's ring, as well as the day each will come into the store to pick it up.

1. The customer who ordered the white gold ring will pick his up the day before the person who bought a diamond ring, which will be picked up the day before the ruby ring (which wasn't ordered by George).

2. Between Clark and the customer who bought the ruby ring, one is coming in on Thursday and the other chose a yellow gold band.

3. The titanium ring (which isn't scheduled for a Tuesday pick-up) has three enormous emeralds set into it.

4. The last of the 5 customers to pick up their ring chose a yellow gold band.

5. Martin will come into the shop to pick up his ring one day before Humphrey, who won't be coming in on Wednesday.

6. The platinum ring doesn't have amethysts in it and won't be picked up on Thursday.

7. The ruby ring will be picked up sometime after the silver ring.

		Bernie	Clark	Humphrey	George	Martin	platinum	silver	titanium	white gold	yellow gold	amethyst	diamond	emerald	ruby	sapphire
Pick-Ups	Monday															
	Tuesday															
	Wednesday															
	Thursday															
	Friday															
Stones	amethyst															
	diamond															
	emerald															
	ruby															
	sapphire															
Metals	platinum															
	silver															
	titanium															
	white gold															
	yellow gold															

Pick-Ups	Customers	Metals	Stones
Monday			
Tuesday			
Wednesday			
Thursday			
Friday			

119

Answers on page 186.

SAY WHAT?

Below is a group of words that, when properly arranged in the blanks, reveal a quote from George A. Romero.

scariest always next horror neighbors real that

I've _____ felt that the _____ _____ is _____ door to us, _____ the _____ monsters are our_____.

CRACK THE PASSWORD

Investigators found a set of possible smartphone passwords at the scene of a crime. But in addition to being scrambled, each word below is missing the same letter. Discover the missing letter, then unscramble the words.

IRONIC

FOULER

PIANOS

Answers on page 186.

FIND THE SUSPECT

You're tracking down a criminal, but rain has swept through the entire county, flooding all the bridges indicated by circles. Your job is to travel to each location—A through I, in any order—by restoring only 2 of the bridges.

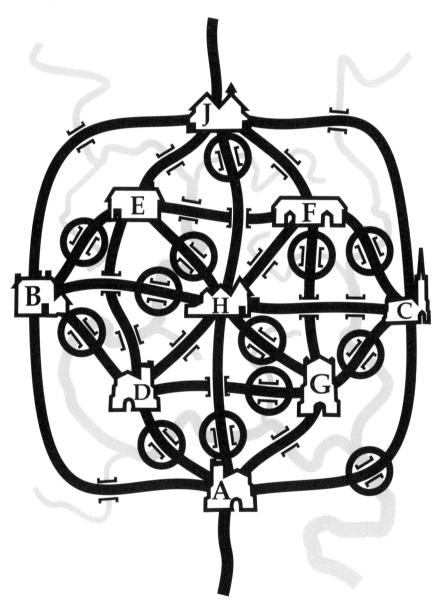

Answers on page 186.

SLITHERLINK PATH

Create a single continuous path along the dotted lines. The path does not cross itself or touch at any corners. Numbers indicate how many line segments surround each cell. We've filled in some line segments to get you started.

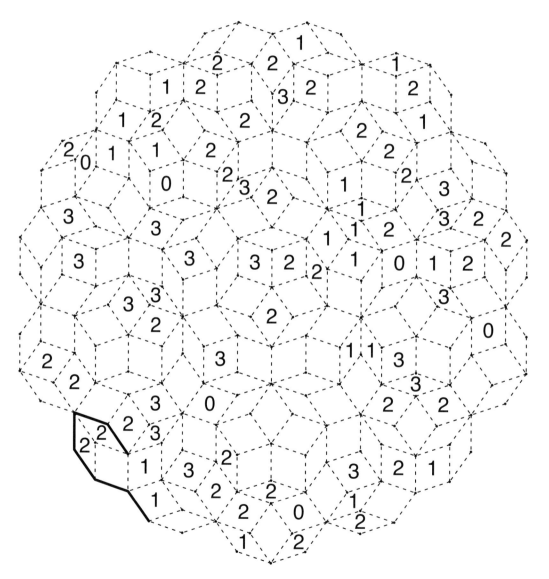

Answers on page 186.

MISSING DETAILS

One detail from each soldier is missing. Can you find which detail is missing in each?

123

CLASS SCHEDULE

The detective has been given a list of teachers he needs to interview at a school that's had a theft. But his list has gotten confused, and now he doesn't know which teachers can be found in which room, or what they teach. Although each item is in the correct column, only 1 item in each column is correctly positioned.

The following facts are true about the correct positions:

1. Neither Art nor Kettering is sixth.

2. Room D5 is 2 places below Harrison and one above Biology.

3. Jones is not in room E9 and is not directly above or below Irving in the list.

4. Room B1 is 3 places below Jones and 2 below English.

5. Room A2 is 1 place below Irving and one above Chemistry.

Can you find the correct subject, teacher, and room for each line?

	Subject	Teacher	Room
1	Art	Gates	A2
2	Biology	Harrison	B1
3	Chemistry	Irving	C8
4	History	Jones	D5
5	English	Kettering	E9
6	Geography	Lee	F7

Answers on page 187.

TALKING TERMINOLOGY

How much do you know about the vocabulary of crime scene investigation? Answer the following questions.

1. What is the difference between a coroner and a medical examiner?

   A. No difference. These are two different terms for the same role.

   B. Coroners are elected and may not be physicians; medical examiners are physicians appointed to the job.

   C. Medical examiners can only perform exams like blood tests and visual examinations, while autopsies must be performed by coroners.

2. In American law, the terms robbery, burglary, and theft are used to describe `three slightly different crimes. Which statement below describes each crime?

   A. This term refers to the act of wrongfully taking property from someone without their consent.

   B. If you use force or the threat of force to take someone else's property without consent, this term is used.

   C. If you enter a structure or dwelling with the intent of committing a crime, this term is used.

3. A forensic dentist is also called by this term.

   A. Entomologist

   B. Odontologist

   C. Pathologist

4. This word is used by arson investigators to describe a substance that promotes or spreads a fire.

   A. Accelerant

   B. Combustant

   C. Flammable

Answers on page 187.

REPLICANTS

Use the 4 tiles given to complete the missing two words in the sentence. Each word uses all four tiles.

Investigators look carefully at the FOR_ _S_ _   _V_D_ _ _ _ in each case.

ADDAGRAM

This puzzle functions exactly like an anagram with an added step: In addition to being scrambled, each word below is missing the same letter. Discover the missing letter, then unscramble the words to reveal five terms related to crime scene investigation.

LOSE _____

NEED ICE _____

EAT SING TIE _____

TEE EDICT _____

HE TIES _____

Answers on page 187.

MOTEL HIDEOUT

A thief hides out in one of the 45 motel rooms listed in the chart below. The motel's in-house detective received a sheet of four clues, signed "The Holiday Thief." Using these clues, the detective found the room number within 15 minutes—but by that time, the thief had fled. Can you find the thief's motel room quicker?

1. It is not a prime number.
2. The first digit is odd, and the second even.
3. It is divisible by 6.
4. The sum of its digits is less than 9.

51	52	53	54	55	56	57	58	59
41	42	43	44	45	46	47	48	49
31	32	33	34	35	36	37	38	39
21	22	23	24	25	26	27	28	29
11	12	13	14	15	16	17	18	19

Answers on page 187.

EAVESDROPPING LOGIC

You overhear a boy and girl arguing. "I knew you knew all about it!" she shouts at him, "but you didn't know that I knew that, did you?" "Actually I did, I just didn't let on that I knew," he replies irritably. The girl is obviously shocked to hear this.

Presuming they are both expressing their
honest opinions, which of the following is not true?

A. He didn't know that she knew that he knew that she knew all about it.

B. He knew that she knew that he knew all about it.

C. She didn't know that he knew that she knew that he knew all about it.

D. Two or more of the above.

EAVESDROPPING LOGIC

John overhears Barbara and Carol discussing something about their friends David and Edward. They seem to be in agreement about what took place between the boys, but not about the rights and wrongs of the situation. John knows everybody concerned and feels a lot more sure than either Barbara or Carol about the morality of what happened.

Which is the least certain of the following?

A. Some people do not believe that everybody acted morally in the situation

B. It is unclear who is certain about the morality of what took place

C. It is unclear whether anything immoral took place

D. It is unclear who knows the most about what happened

Answers on page 187.

IT'S IN THE BLOOD (PART 1)

Information about blood types can help investigators narrow down who could have left blood at the scene of a crime. Read the following information about blood types, then turn the page for a quiz.

Scientists have discovered eight major blood types; some are compatible, but others are not.

1. O+: 38 percent

O+ blood is needed more often than any other blood type because it's the most common. O+ blood can be given to a person with A+, B+, AB+, or O+ blood. A person with O+ blood can receive blood from O+ or O- donors.

2. A+: 34 percent

A person with A+ blood can receive A+, A-, O+, or O- blood. However, A+ blood can be given only to a person with the A+ or AB+ blood types.

3. B+: 9 percent

B+ blood can be given only to those with either AB+ or B+ blood. This blood type can receive blood from B+, B-, O+, or O- donors.

4. O-: 7 percent

O- is considered the universal donor because it can be given to anyone, regardless of blood type. However, a person with the O- blood type can receive blood only from other O- donors.

5. A-: 6 percent

A- blood can be given to a person with AB-, A-, AB+, or A+. This blood type can only receive blood from O- or A- donors.

6. AB+: 3 percent

AB+ is considered a universal receiver because people with this blood type can receive blood of any type. But AB+ blood can only be given to a person who also has AB+ blood.

7. B-: 2 percent

B- blood can be given to those with B-, AB-, B+, or AB+ blood. A person with B- blood can receive blood from O- or B- blood types.

8. AB-: 1 percent

AB- is the least common blood type. A person with this type can give blood to AB+ or AB- blood types, but must receive blood from O-, A-, B-, and AB- blood types.

IT'S IN THE BLOOD (PART II)

(Do not read this until you have read the previous page!)

1. Which blood type is more common?

   ☐ A+   ☐ B-

2. Is O positive or O negative the universal donor?

   ☐ O+   ☐ O-

3. People with this blood type are considered the universal recipient.

   ☐ A-   ☐ AB+   ☐ AB-   ☐ O+

4. This is the least common blood type.

   ☐ A-   ☐ AB+   ☐ AB-   ☐ O+

5. People with O + blood can receive blood from O- donors.

   ☐ TRUE   ☐ FALSE

Answers on page 187.

WITNESS STATEMENT

On Box Street, there are 5 adjacent houses that are identical to each other. You need to interview Mr. Stark, but without any addresses on the doors you are not sure which house to approach. At the local coffee shop, you ask the waitress for help. She is able to provide the following information:

A. There are always decorations in House B's windows and in one of the houses adjacent to it.

B. Mr. Stark hates decorations.

C. The occupants of House E keep to themselves.

D. Mr. Stark's girlfriend lives in House C, but they don't live together.

E. Mr. Stark and his girlfriend think alike in all regards.

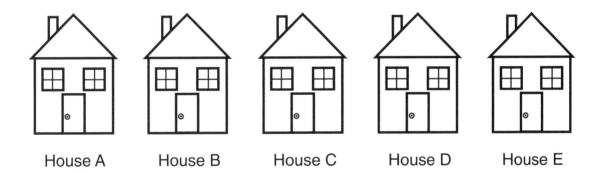

House A   House B   House C   House D   House E

Answers on page 187.

KNOT PROBLEM

How many rings of string are in the diagram: 1, 2, 3, or more? Are they linked together? Which one of them contains a knot?

KNOT PROBLEM

Which piece of string—A, B, or C—would knot up if you pulled on it?

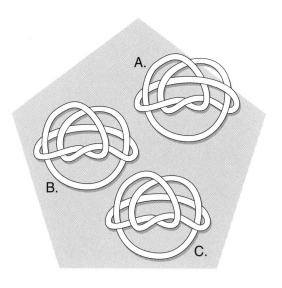

132

Answers on page 187.

GAME BOARD (PART I)

Study this game board for one minute, particularly the shapes and their placement. Then turn the page for a memory challenge.

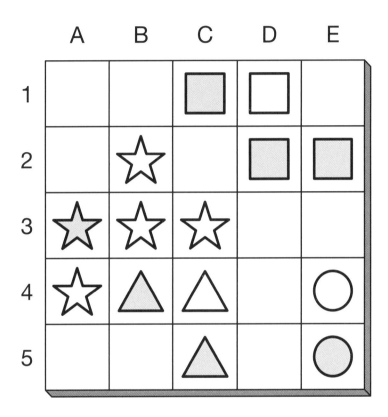

GAME BOARD (PART II)

Do not read this until you have read the previous page!

Duplicate the board as seen on the previous page.

	A	B	C	D	E
1					
2					
3					
4					
5					

Answers on page 188.

SYMBOLS OF OZ (PART I)

The victim of the crime was an Australia buff. Photographs of these items were found at the crime scene. Study the page for a minute, then turn the page for a memory challenge.

Koala

Boomerang

Kangaroo

Ayers Rock

Platypus

Emu

Australian flag

Great Barrier Reef

SYMBOLS OF OZ (PART II)

Do not look at this until you have read the previous page!

Check off the items you saw on the previous page.

SYDNEY OPERA HOUSE

KANGAROO

WOMBAT

BOOMERANG

WALKABOUT

AUSTRALIAN FLAG

EMU

OUTBACK

CROCODILE DUNDEE

BILLABONG

KOALA

AYERS ROCK

WALTZING MATILDA

Answers on page 188.

CANVASS THE BUILDING

To search for potential witnesses to the crime, start at the top left corner, visits each corner exactly once, and end back at the same corner on the map of the office building.

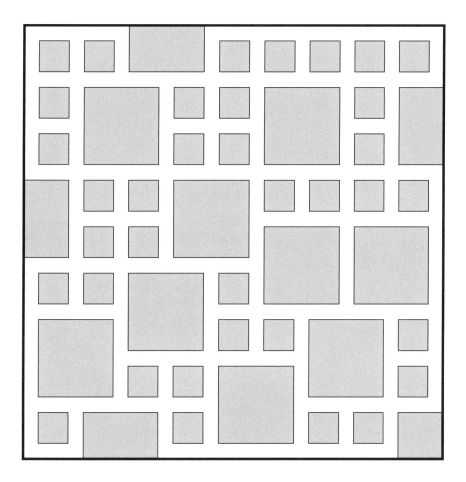

Answers on page 188.

CRACK THE PASSWORD

You've found a list of the criminal's passwords. But in addition to being scrambled, each word below is missing the same letter. Discover the missing letter, then unscramble the words to reveal the passwords.

COMETS

BLARED

FORMAL

THEIRS

CRACK THE PASSWORD

You've found a list of the criminal's passwords. But in addition to being scrambled, each word below is missing the same letter. Discover the missing letter, then unscramble the words to reveal the passwords.

AMPERE

FEISTY

GORILY

Answers on page 188.

WHAT DO YOU SEE? (PART I)

Study this picture of the crime scene for 1 minute, then turn the page.

WHAT DO YOU SEE? (PART II)

(Do not read this until you have read the previous page!)

1. The knickknacks on the fireplace had been knocked over.

☐ **TRUE**   ☐ **FALSE**

2. Each small placard around the body indicates a bullet.
How many were there?

A. 1

B. 2

C. 3

D. 4

3. A splotch of blood was found on the cushion of the window seat.

☐ **TRUE**   ☐ **FALSE**

4. A lamp was knocked over.

☐ **TRUE**   ☐ **FALSE**

5. Both chairs in the scene were knocked over.

☐ **TRUE**   ☐ **FALSE**

Answers on page 188.

QUICK CRIME QUIZ

How much do you know about the history of crime scene investigation? Answer the following questions.

1. If the crime scene technicians did not find a person's fingerprint at the scene of a crime, does that prove that person couldn't have been there?

☐ **YES**   ☐ **NO**

2. Is "body farm" another word for morgue?

☐ **YES**   ☐ **NO**

3. Can a guilty person fool a polygraph test?

☐ **YES**   ☐ **NO**

4. Can an innocent person fail a polygraph test?

☐ **YES**   ☐ **NO**

5. What does the acronym AFIS stand for?

☐ **ARSON FEDERAL INVESTIGATOR AT THE SCENE**

☐ **AUTOMATED FINGERPRINT IDENTIFICATION SYSTEM**

☐ **AUTOMATIC FACIAL IDENTIFICATION SYSTEM**

Answers on page 188.

A CASE OF ARSON (PART I)

Read the account of the crime, then turn to page 144 to answer questions.

On Saturday December 9th at 3:17 AM, a passing trucker made a call to 911 to report a blaze at a structure on Faraday Road. (Faraday Road is in an office park; the trucker was on route 56, which runs parallel.) Firefighters, on arriving, found a fire at the empty office building at 514 E. Faraday Road. It had not yet spread to the surrounding office buildings. Building owned by PilotBuilding Enterprises. The office building houses three businesses: one dentist's office (Dr. Thomas Wexworth, DDS); one app developer (Games to Infinity); one therapists' office (Dr. Wendy Yaxley, PhD; Dr. Rashida Brown, PhD). Each renter had five rooms (entry room, three offices, bathroom) and one storage closet.

The blaze was set in the app developer's office, specifically the storage closet. It spread throughout the office and through the shared wall to the dentist's office, which incurred extensive damage in one room and minimal damage in the others. It did not affect the therapists' office other than some smoke and water damage.

The app developer was a local branch of a larger company. Four employees worked out of this branch: Tomas Villanueva, lead developer; Rembert Whitehead, audio developer; Rachel Smith, junior developer; Yvette Washington, marketing. Another junior developer had been recently fired for cause: Thomas Greene.

The building owner provided cleaning once a week. Cleaning supplies for small spills were kept in the bathroom cabinet. All four employees interviewed attested that the storage closet was used minimally, primarily for paper materials, and that they could not remember chemicals or flammable materials being housed there.

Further investigation revealed that turpentine was used as an accelerant; all employees agreed that none was found anywhere in the office.

There were no signs of forced entry. The external door to the building and the main door to each set of offices were opened by electronic keycard. Current keycards were in the possession of current employees, the building owner, and the cleaning crew.

Attention focused on current and ex-employees of the app developers. All professed to be happy with their employment and to work well together. Washington brought up an ex-boyfriend (Tim Tresworth, one charge of drunk and disorderly at age 21, one dropped charge of shoplifting at the age of 22, no record of arson) who had gotten "borderline stalkery" when they broke up 6 months ago. She had broken up with him partly because he had previously accused her of spending too much time at work and flirting with her male colleagues. He no longer had access to her keycard, but he would have had access to her purse while they were dating, and might have duplicated it then.

When interviewed, Tresworth expressed anger at Washington for "trying to get him involved." He attested that she "went crazy" after their breakup and accused him of stalking her when he was just trying to return some items. He was "dating someone right now" and "didn't need to be reminded of his crazy ex." He professed to have been at her house the night of the fire. His current girlfriend, Janet Parkinson, confirmed. She also said (after asking that "this not get back to him") that she could see him doing something stupid ("he, uh, doesn't have great impulse control") right after a breakup, but she couldn't see him doing something that required a lot of planning 6 months after a breakup. ("Like, he wouldn't plan ahead and get her keycard or anything. He might, like, bang on the door to her office building to yell at her or those guys.")

Thomas Greene, former employee, no prior convictions, was let go for not meeting deadlines, not responding well to feedback, and not working well with outside clients. Greene said that he had not been given clear directions or support and that he'd been set up to fail, and that by the time he was fired he was glad to leave the company. He had since been doing freelance work. He had turned in his keycard to Villanueva (Villanueva confirmed).

A half-full container of turpentine was found in his apartment, in a closet in the guest bedroom, behind a stack of blank canvases. He attested that it was left behind from a girlfriend who had painted oils. There was no dust on the canister; no fingerprints were found.

A CASE OF ARSON (PART II)

(Do not read this until you have read the previous page!)

1. The fire could have been accidental.

   ☐ LIKELY   ☐ UNLIKELY

2. There were signs of forced entry.

   ☐ TRUE   ☐ UNCONFIRMED   ☐ FALSE

3. Thomas Greene had a working keycard for the building.

   ☐ TRUE   ☐ UNCONFIRMED   ☐ FALSE

4. Tresworth had an alibi for the time of the crime.

   ☐ TRUE   ☐ UNCONFIRMED   ☐ FALSE

5. The turpentine found in Greene's apartment was left behind by an ex-girlfriend.

   ☐ TRUE   ☐ UNCONFIRMED   ☐ FALSE

Answers on page 188.

AFTERNOON ICE CREAM

On Friday afternoon, Sally and her friends, Emily and Helen, went to Frank's ice cream stand for an after-school snack. The girls had a hard time deciding which flavor to get, so they each decided on a different one. Using the codes below, determine what each friend ordered and which ice cream flavor they chose.

1. Emily had trouble making up her mind, but she didn't just order a cone.

2. Helen didn't get vanilla ice cream.

3. The one who ordered the sundae also selected coffee ice cream.

4. Sally ordered a frappe, but she didn't get chocolate ice cream.

Name	Ordered	Flavor

Answers on page 188.

SHE'S A COP!

Find the answers in the grid in which police drama you would see the list of actresses. (Hint: this list is in alphabetical order of the TV show titles). Every word listed is contained within the group of letters. Words can be found in a straight line horizontally, vertically, or diagonally. They may be read either forward or backward.

Kathryn Morris as Lilly Rush

Marg Helgenberger as Catherine Willows

Mary McCormack as Mary Shannon

Mariska Hargitay as Olivia Benson

Vivica A. Fox as Nicole Scott

Angie Dickinson as Suzanne "Pepper" Anderson

Holly Hunter as Grace Hanadarko

Heather Locklear as Stacy Sheridan

Kyra Sedgwick as Brenda Leigh Johnson

Peggy Lipton as Julie Barnes

Poppy Montgomery as Samantha Spade

```
C T M D N R E L T O T I C E W
L S H P O L E J S D I O L I P
R A A G W M H S R C D A T W O
P C W T I O I S O A C H U I L
I O Q A O S V S U L O S E T I
S H L K N S N Q S U C C O S C
T H E I P D S I T I A E C O E
E R C I C D O A A R N G H U W
P S A P O E T R G L S G T T R
O E A M H R W G D P P W H M T
L H E C A O N O U E Q N E I H
I H W C D I L C M O R C I S O
T C E H V L T J H A N S A S U
I I I A I C O T E C N S V I S
A C S L N P L C W I T H O U W
```

147

HOCKEY LEGENDS

The Anaheim Community center hosted this year's annual fundraiser for the local children's hospital, which featured more than a dozen different legendary ice hockey players. The event assigned each player to a different booth, where they would charge a fee for both autographs and photos, with all proceeds going directly to the children's hospital. Jason and his brother Derrick were among the first in line, and they both purchased photos and autographs from 5 different players. Using only the clues below, figure out the price charged by each player for their autograph and photo, as well as which booth they were assigned to during the event.

1. Jim Janelle charged $30 for his photograph.

2. Between Rick Rogers and the player who charged $35 per autograph, one was in booth #3 and the other charged more for his photograph than any other of the 5.

3. Of Uri Ulner and the hockey legend who charged $75 per photo, one charged just $15 per autograph and the other was in booth #7.

4. The player who wanted $55 per photo charged less for his autograph than the hockey legend who wanted $40 per photo.

5. The player who charged the least amount of money for his autograph wasn't in booth #12.

6. Of Chip Caitlin (who didn't charge $40 for his photo) and the player who charged $50 per autograph, one was in booth #10 and the other in booth #12.

7. The player in booth #12 didn't charge $75 per photo.

8. The player with the most expensive autograph charged only $30 per photo.

9. Neither Chip Caitlin nor the player in booth #10 charged $20 per photograph.

10. Of the 5 hockey legends Jason and Derrick saw, the one with the $15 autograph offered the most expensive photo.

Autograph Price	Player	Booth Number	Photo Price
$10			
$15			
$25			
$35			
$50			

		Player					Booth Number					Photo Price				
		Chip Caitlin	Dan Dalton	Jim Janelle	Rick Rogers	Uri Ulner	booth #3	booth #6	booth #7	booth #10	booth #12	$20	$30	$40	$55	$75
Autograph Price	$10															
	$15															
	$25															
	$35															
	$50															
Photo Price	$20															
	$30															
	$40															
	$55															
	$75															
Booth Number	booth #3															
	booth #6															
	booth #7															
	booth #10															
	booth #12															

Answers on page 189.

FINGERPRINT MATCH

Find the matching fingerprint(s). There may be more than one.

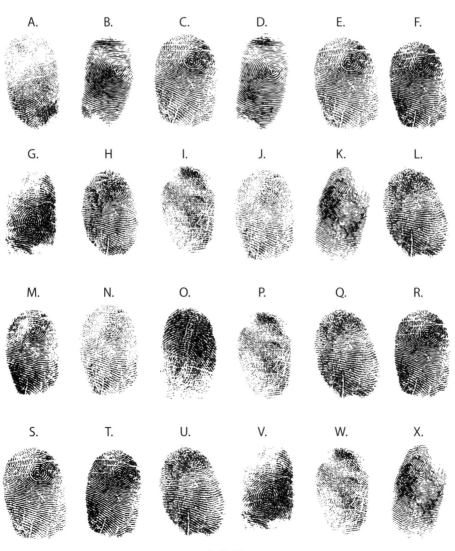

Answers on page 189.

PLANTED EVIDENCE AT THE SCENE

Change just one letter on each line to go from the top word to the bottom word. Do not change the order of the letters. You must have a common English word at each step.

PLANT

_____

_____

_____

SCENE

ELEVATOR WORDS

Like an elevator, words move up and down the "floors" of this puzzle. Starting with the first answer, the second part of each answer carries down to become the first part of the following answer. With the clues given, complete the puzzle.

1. An uptick in crime incidents
2. A graphic image of a wave's frequency
3. Companies send these
4. A company logo shows up on this
5. Holds hair back from your face
6. Grade school music classes might teach this
7. Groupies are part of this.

1. Crime _____
2. _____
3. _____ _____
4. _____
5. _____
6. _____ _____
7. _____ scene

Answers on page 189.

ON YOUR MARK, GET SET...

Go! And be sure to find the 10 differences between these scenes along the way.

Answers on page 189.

PLAYMAKER (PART I)

Study this locker room scene for 2 minutes before turning the page for a memory challenge.

PLAYMAKER (PART II)

Do read this until you have read the previous page!

Of the following plays, which is identical to the one you saw on the previous page?

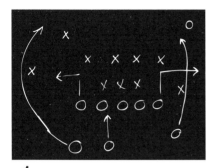

5.

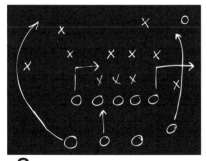

3.

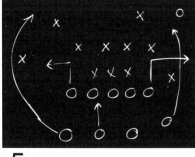

1.

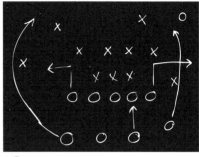

6.

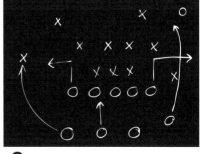

4.

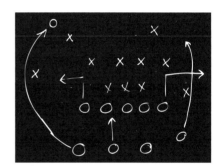

2.

Answers on page 189.

GAME BOARD (PART I)

Study this game board for one minute, particularly the shapes and their placement. Then turn the page for a memory challenge.

	A	B	C	D	E
1	★				■
2		■	○		
3				☆	
4		●			
5	△				▲

GAME BOARD (PART II)

Do not read this until you have read the previous page!

Duplicate the board as seen on the previous page.

	A	B	C	D	E
1					
2					
3					
4					
5					

Answers on page 190.

CRACK THE PASSWORD

You've found a list of the criminal's passwords. But in addition to being scrambled, each word below is missing the same letter. Discover the missing letter, then unscramble the words to reveal the passwords.

ALPINE

ELOPED

SPREES

CRACK THE PASSWORD

You've found a list of the criminal's passwords. But in addition to being scrambled, each word below is missing the same letter. Discover the missing letter, then unscramble the words to reveal the passwords.

ACHIER

PIRACY

EERIER

157

Answers on page 190.

ROYAL CARTOGRAPHERS

The tiny 17th century kingdom of Wertenmarchte, though all but forgotten today, was world-renowned for its beautiful, hand-illustrated maps. Every Wertenmarchten king appointed a royal cartographer who was in charge of creating and updating the kingdom's collection. Five master cartographers were employed by various kings between 1624 and 1691, and any of those maps can regularly fetch more than $100,000 each. Incredibly, 5 different maps, one from each of the 5 masters, went up for sale last week at the annual cartographic auction in Edinburgh. Using the clues and charts below, match each of the 5 masters to the years in which they served as royal cartographer, and determine what area of the globe each map represented and how much each map sold for at auction.

1. Between Penniford Penstrent's map and the one that sold for the second-highest price, one focused only on Europe and the other was a complete world map.

2. Lubrecht Laliane served as royal cartographer just before the cartographer whose map sold for $116,000.

3. The 5 maps that went up for auction today are one from Guy Gaulois (who never made any European maps), one from Lubrecht Laliane, the world map (which didn't fetch the highest price of all 5 maps), the one that sold for $125,000, and the one from the royal cartographer who served the King of Wertenmarchte for 7 years.

4. Between the world map and the Asian map, one was done by Ivan Irinaise and the other was handcrafted by the last Wertenmarchte royal cartographer (who wasn't Denis Dupuys).

5. The cartographer who crafted the Asian map served the King of Wertenmarchte just before the one who created the map of Africa.

6. The map that sold for less than its expected price of $100,000 was done by Penniford Penstrent's immediate Wertenmarchten predecessor.

		Dupuys	Gaulois	Irinaise	Laliane	Penstrent	Africa	Americas	Asia	Europe	World	$85,000	$116,000	$125,000	$144,000	$273,000
Careers	1624-1645															
	1645-1652															
	1652-1676															
	1676-1680															
	1680-1691															
Auction Prices	$85,000															
	$116,000															
	$125,000															
	$144,000															
	$273,000															
Map Areas	Africa															
	Americas															
	Asia															
	Europe															
	World															

Careers	Cartographers	Map Areas	Auction Prices
1624-1645			
1645-1652			
1652-1676			
1676-1680			
1680-1691			

Answers on page 190.

CRACK THE CODE

The 8 symbols each represent a different number between 1 and 10. The numbers to the right and below the grid show the totals of that row or column. Can you deduce the numerical value of each symbol?

Answers on page 190.

GLOBE QUEST

You're tracking down an interstate criminal, following him around the country. You know he'll visit 9 cities that host his criminal enterprises, and (fortunately for your agency's budget) that he'll try to find the cheapest flights. What route do you anticipate him taking?

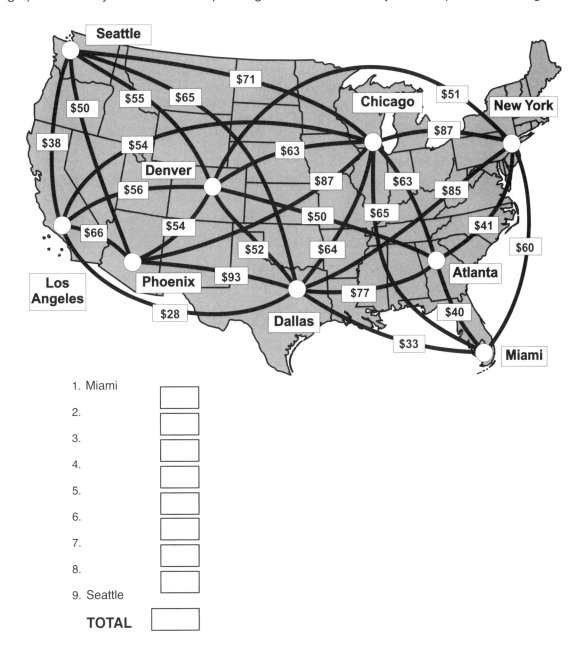

1. Miami

2.

3.

4.

5.

6.

7.

8.

9. Seattle

TOTAL

Answers on page 190.

SCIENTISTS

How well do you know your scientists? We've described 15 scientists here, and given you their first name and last initial. See if you can figure out their last names, and then find them in the word search grid. Names can be found in a straight line horizontally, vertically, or diagonally. They may read either forward or backward.

1. Seventeenth century French mathematician and physicist who is perhaps best known for his philosophical statement: "I think, therefore I am."

Rene _____

2. Danish physicist who won the Nobel Prize in 1922 for his contributions to the field of quantum mechanics. He was also deeply involved in the Manhattan Project.

Niels _____

3. Nineteenth century French chemist who created the first vaccine for rabies and anthrax, and who invented a process for sterilizing milk which would later be named after him.

Louis _____

4. Renaissance-era Polish astronomer and priest who established the first comprehensive theory placing the sun at the center of the solar system, instead of the Earth.

Nicolaus _____

5. Nobel Prize winning German physicist (1918) who is generally recognized as the founder of quantum theory.

Max _____

6. German theoretical physicist who won the Nobel Prize in 1921 for his discovery of the photoelectric effect, but who is more widely known for his special theory of relativity.

Albert _____

7. English physicist, mathematician and astronomer who developed differential and integral calculus and first described universal gravitation and the 3 laws of motion.

Sir Isaac _____

8. To many people, he was the embodiment of the Italian Renaissance man: an artist, scientist, anatomist, engineer, and inventor, perhaps best known for his painting, the Mona Lisa.

Leonardo _____

9. Nineteenth century English naturalist who wrote "On the Origin of Species" and was the first to describe natural selection.

Charles _____

10. Ancient Greek mathematician, engineer and inventor who gave the first extremely accurate approximation of pi, and who invented a famous screw pump which bears his name.

A _____

162

11. Founding Father of the United States whose many inventions included bifocals and the lightning rod. He first suggested flying a kite in a thunderstorm as a way of providing that lightning was a form of electricity in 1750.

Benjamin _____

12. Polish-born French chemist and physicist who was a pioneer in the field of radioactivity. She was also the first person to win 2 Nobel Prizes.

Marie _____

13. German mathematician and astronomer who established laws of planetary motion which are now named after him.

Johannes _____

14. English chemist and physicist whose experiments confirmed the existence of electromagnetic fields. He also discovered benzene and invented the Bunsen burner.

Michael _____

15. Serbian engineer and inventor who revolutionized the field of electromagnetism in the late nineteenth century. He pioneered the use of alternating current that helped to usher in the modern use of electronics.

Nikola _____

```
U N I W R A D A V I N C I E W
F A R A D A Y N R L V B S I R
G J V H G L L R I G W E P U U
Q F R C U V I H R E V X U N E
A J P G O H F O W O T R M E T
C D S R T P Z B J V Y S N Q S
P U E N P J E R B B Y E N J A
T N M S O L E R S Z W Y C I P
E I E E C L A A N T W I R I E
S L K U P A R N O I Q R C I L
L K J E N U R N C F C R C S S
A N K V H E L T N K R U J H N
Q A W X Q P F A E Q Q W S K N
S R W K N Y A M U S C U R I E
Q F A R C H I M E D E S I J K
```

Answers on page 190.

SPY FLY

As an international spy, your mission is to travel from your headquarters at Seth Castle to your safe house at Faro. To disguise your trail, you must stop once—and only once—at each airport. See if you can find the cheapest route for your trip. Less than $240 would make you a Steady Sleuth; less than $230, a Cool Operator; less than $220, a Crafty Agent. If you can make it on $200, then you're a Super Spy!

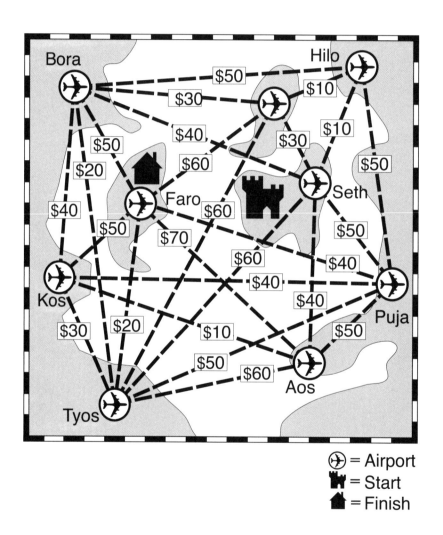

= Airport
= Start
= Finish

Answers on page 191.

ACRONYM QUIZ (PART I)

Read the following information about acronyms used in forensic science, then turn the page for a quiz.

AAFS: American Academy of Forensic Sciences

ABO: ABO blood group system

ADME: absorption, distribution, metabolism, and excretion

ALS: alternate light source

ASTM: American Society for Testing Materials

BAC: blood alcohol concentration

CE: capillary electrophoresis

FID: flame ionization detector for gas chromatography

GLP: good laboratory practice

GSR: gunshot residue

MO: modus operandi

NASH: natural, accidental, suicidal, homicidal (cause of death)

PDQ: paint data query

RMNE: random man not excluded

ACRONYM QUIZ (PART II)

(Do not read this until you have read the previous page!)

1. In the context of forensic investigation, PDQ stands for:
   A. pretty darn quick
   B. paint data query, a database of vehicle paint colors
   C. people deserve quality

2. GLP stands for:
   A. gunshot
   B. guided laser probe
   C. good laboratory practice

3. The professional society for people in the forensic professions is:
   A. American Academy of Forensic Sciences (AAFS)
   B. Academy of American Forensic Investigators (AAFI)
   C. American Society for Forensic Professionals (ASFP)

4. Light sources such as ultraviolet and fluorescent light are referred to as:
   A. unfamiliar light sources (ULS)
   B. alternate light sources (ALS)
   C. non-standard light sources (NSLS)

5. Pharmaceutical compounds go through four phases:
   A. absorption, distribution, metabolism, and excretion (ADME)
   B. ingestion, distribution, affect, excretion (IDAE)
   C. ingestion, metabolism, distribution, absorption (IMDA)

Answers on page 191.

FIND THE SUSPECT

You're tracking down a suspect, but rain has swept through the entire county, flooding all the bridges indicated by circles. Your job is to travel to each location—A through I, in any order—by restoring only 2 of the bridges.

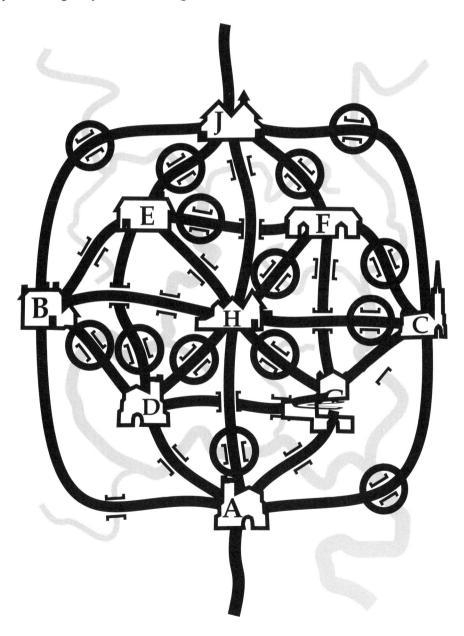

Answers on page 191.

LOCKER ROOM

The game may be over, but there is still plenty of action! There are 15 differences in the illustrations below. See if you can find them all.

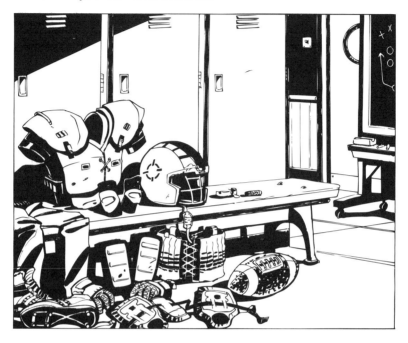

Answers on page 191.

PRIME SUSPECT

The police have drawn up a list of prime suspect descriptions for a recent bank robbery. However, due to a clerical error, although each item is in the correct column, only one entry in each column is correctly positioned. The following facts are true about the correct order.

1. Yellow is one row below medium and somewhere above mauve.

2. Thin is 2 rows above Spanish.

3. Hunched is 3 places below English.

4. White is somewhere above dark and 2 places above fat.

5. Italian is 2 places above purple.

6. Brown is one row below both yellow and African.

7. Cream is immediately below purple but 3 places below none.

Can you find the correct nationality, hair color, coat color, and build for each suspect?

	Nationality	Hair	Coat	Build
1	English	none	green	slim
2	Italian	white	yellow	thin
3	Spanish	red	mauve	fat
4	Mexican	gray	blue	round
5	African	brown	purple	medium
6	Chinese	dark	cream	hunched

Answers on page 191.

CURRENCY QUIZ

You've found an assortment of currency from foreign countries on a search of the criminal's house. How well do you know your currencies? Many countries use the same name for their currency. Find the country that doesn't belong in each list.

Countries whose currency is called the franc:

A. French Polynesia

B. France

C. Gabon

D. Madagascar

Countries whose currency is called the dollar:

A. Namibia

B. Singapore

C. Zimbabwe

D. Iraq

Countries whose currency is called the pound:

A. Switzerland

B. Cyprus

C. Egypt

D. Gibraltar

Countries whose currency is called the shilling:

A. United Kingdom

B. Tanzania

C. Uganda

D. Kenya

Countries whose currency is called the dinar:

A. Algeria

B. Bahrain

C. Jordan

D. Albania

Countries whose currency is called the rupee:

A. Sri Lanka

B. Bangladesh

C. India

D. Pakistan

Countries whose currency is called the peso:

A. Paraguay

B. Philippines

C. Argentina

D. Chile

Answers on page 191.

SPY FLY

As an international spy, your mission is to travel from your headquarters at Seth Castle to your safe house at Faro. To disguise your trail, you must stop once--and only once--at each airport. See if you can find the cheapest route for your trip. Less than $310 would make you a Steady Sleuth; less than $300, a Cool Operator; less than $290, a Crafty Agent. If you can make it on $280, then you're a Super Spy!

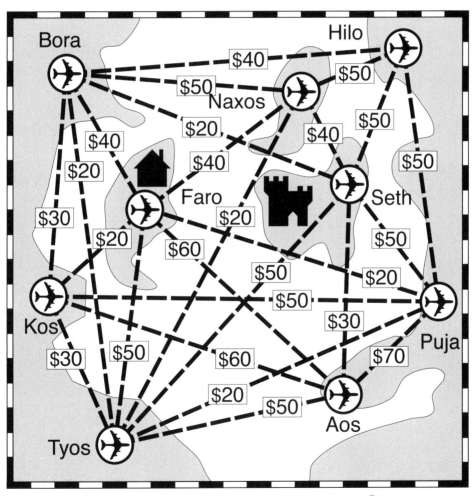

= Airport
= Start
= Finish

Answers on page 192.

THE LAW

Every legal term listed is contained within the group of letters. Words can be found in a straight line horizontally, vertically, or diagonally. They may be read either forward or backward.

APPEAL	FINE
ARRAIGN	HEARING
CIVIL	JUDGE
COURT	JURY
DAMAGES	LAWYER
DISCOVERY	PLEA
DISMISS	RECORD
DOCUMENT	RULING
EVIDENCE	SENTENCE
FELONY	TRANSCRIPT

```
A E A Y B M V X H Q F W Y Z Y
T E U E V K S H D D P V V R S
R M L A V E A P P E A L U X S
U A G P G I H X T V W J A G I
O R A A J I D J R A E U N F M
C R M P B R U E A C Z D L E S
L A D O C U M E N T I G O L I
D I I A W T Q E S C V E Z O D
R G S E H F T S C Y E T T N E
R N C L D N V F R A S L Q Y V
E J O I E N D I I D R O C E R
Y A V S R E H N P R U L I N G
W O E U P P Q E T C Z I B Y J
A G R T F Y F N R U C I V I L
L L Y H O M F G N I R A E H S
```

Answers on page 192.

SLITHERLINK PATH

Create a single continuous path along the dotted lines. The path does not cross itself or touch at any corners. Numbers indicate how many line segments surround each cell. We've filled in some line segments to get you started.

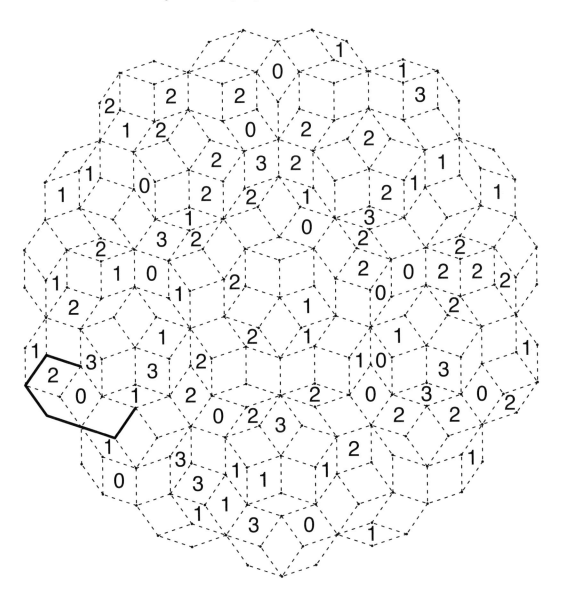

Answers on page 192.

ANSWERS

FROM CLUES TO TRIAL (PAGE 4)
Answers may vary. CLUES, flues, flies, fries, tries, tried, triad, TRIAL

COME TOGETHER (PAGE 4)

| S | U | S | P | E | C | T | E | D |

| E | X | A | M | I | N | E | R | S |

| B | A | L | L | I | S | T | I | C |

CRIME STINKS (PAGE 5)
Answers may vary. CRIME, prime, pride, bride, brine, brink, blink, slink, STINK

CRIME RHYMES (PAGE 5)
1. eel steal; 2. bleu clue; 3. beef thief; 4. lime crime; 5. aperitif thief; 6. yacht plot; 7. reflective detective; 8. mint print

CRIME CRYPTOGRAM (PAGE 6)
The actor's costar accused him of a dastardly crime, but the police refused to investigate. What did he do?
He stole the scene!

MEALTIME CRIME (PAGE 6)
What did the headline read for the bakery theft that took place during the solstice in June?
The summertime key lime crime.

MOTEL HIDEOUT (PAGE 7)
The thief is in room 59.

TYPES OF EVIDENCE (PAGES 8-10)
1. True; 2. False. Palynology is the science that studies plant spores, insects, seeds, and other microorganisms. 3. False. 4. True. 5. True.

BURIED DIAMONDS (PAGE 11)

	Tree	Location	No. Diamonds
1	beech	river	15
2	cedar	garden	10
3	dogwood	lake	8
4	elm	fence	7
5	ash	park	5
6	fir	wood	12

QUICK CRIME QUIZ (PAGE 12)
1. True. Fingerprints were used as signatures as far back as ancient Babylon; 2. Fingerprints; 3. True. Bertillion's system produced a set of measurements for each person (for instance, the length of their head, their middle finger, and their foot) that were, in theory, unique to that person. 4. Mug shots; 5. 1850

CRIMINALS (PAGE 13)
bandit, burglar, crook, gangster, mugger, outlaw, robber, thief

COUNT CASHULA (PAGE 13)
Twelve thousand twelve hundred and twenty-two dollars is $13,222.

MEDICAL EXAMINERS (PAGES 14-15)

ANSWERS

FINGERPRINT MATCH (PAGE 16)
The matching pairs are: A and K; B and E; C and F; D and I; G and L; H and J.

WHAT DO YOU SEE? (PAGES 17-18)
1. Open; 2. False; 3. Chest of drawers; 4. Left hand; 5. No.

STRINGING ALONG (PAGE 19)
Hector gathered some slack in the middle of the string, made a loop, and tied it in a knot. Then he took the scissors and cut the loop, leaving the coffee cup dangling from the knotted string in his hand.

LOGIC: THE MORNING LANDSCAPE
(PAGES 20-21)
His first stop was at the Browns', and on his second stop he planted the maple tree (Clue 3). Both of these addresses had to be Lanes (Clue 3), but the maple tree could not be planted on Maple Lane (Clue 2), so it was planted on Apple Lane, and the Browns lived on Maple Lane. The pear tree was planted at his third stop, and the Whites' house was his last stop of the morning (Clue 4). The pear tree was not planted on Pear Drive, so it was planted on Elm Drive. Pear Drive was the address of the last stop (the Whites' house), where he planted a fruit tree (Clue 2), the apple tree. This leaves the elm tree to be planted at his first stop, at the Browns' house on Maple Lane. Finally, since the Greys did not live on Apple Lane (Clue 1), they lived on Elm Drive, and the Greens had a maple tree planted in their yard on Apple Lane.

In summary:
First Elm tree Brown
Maple Lane
Second Maple tree Green
Apple Lane

Third Pear tree Grey
Elm Drive
Fourth Apple tree White
Pear Drive

SEARCHING FOR EVIDENCE
(PAGES 22-23)

REMEMBERING THE SCENE
(PAGES 24-26)
1. C; 2. False; 3. False; 4. False; 5. B; 6. C

SCIENCE (PAGE 27)
1. b) when it is blue
2. b) a meteorite
3. c) partially blind
4. a) 240,000 miles
5. c) 140,000 hairs

WILD WEST (PAGE 28)

	Name	Surname	Location	Firearm
1	Abel	Garrett	Fort Griffin	Cavalry
2	Drew	Indiana	San Antonio	Peacemaker
3	Earp	James	Red River	Schofield
4	Fingers	Hitchcock	Dodge City	Winchester
5	Butch	Lightning	Colby	Golden Boy
6	Cat	Kid	Ogallala	Derringer

SUPERMARKET SHENANIGANS
(PAGE 29)
Checkout Charlie bought a doughnut and a carton of eggnog. The applesauce cost $2.10, the pound of beef cost $3.30, the bag of candy cost $1.90, the doughnut cost $1.00, and the carton of eggnog cost $3.80.

ANSWERS

:RACK THE PASSWORD (PAGE 29)
Rachel, Monica, Phoebe, Joey, Chandler,
)ss—characters on *Friends.*

HE YELLOW-BRICK ROAD (PAGE 30)
The blue road. If the liar tells us the truth-
ller would say to take the red road, we know
at we should take the blue road. If the truth-
ller tells us the liar would tell us to take the
d road, he's telling the truth that the red road
)uld be lied about as the right way to go. So if
e are told to take the red road, we should take
e blue road and vice versa, regardless of who
e ask.

'ORD LADDER (PAGE 30)
:EK, seed, send, mend, mind, FIND

AVESDROPPING LOGIC (PAGE 31)
e answer is A. B is extremely unlikely, given
at we don't know what injury she has sus-
ned and given the use of the word "fair"
her than "true." C simply agrees with the
I and doesn't qualify her account as "not
actly fair" would suggest. D responds to the
I woman rather than the girl and expects her
have taken the girl's comment into account
fore making her own, which would be impos-
le given the order of speaking in the pas-
ge, and so is essentially nonsensical. A is the
ly reasonable option.

AN A CLUE SET YOU FREE?
.GE 32)
swer may vary. CLUE, glue, glee, flee, FREE

:LL A TALE, GO TO JAIL (PAGE 32)
swers may vary. TALE, tall, pall, pail, JAIL

OTEL HIDEOUT (PAGE 33)
e thief is in room 42.

POISON! (PAGES 34-36)
1. False. 2. False. 3. False. 4. True. 5. True

QUICK CRIME QUIZ (PAGE 37)
1. Juan Vucetich of Argentina created the first
fingerprint classification system for police. 2.
No. 3. Yes. It is rare, but it does happen. 4. Yes.
Wear, certain chemicals, and certain chemo-
therapy drugs can erode fingerprints, but it is
difficult to do. 5. Researchers have been devel-
oping techniques to lift fingerprints off fabric,
but it is more difficult than lifting them from
other materials.

DETECTIVES (PAGES 38-39)
The leftover letters spell: "Sherlock Holmes and
Doctor Watson (Doyle)."

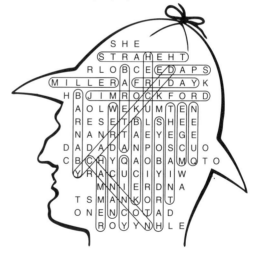

ANSWERS

MECHANIC SHOP (PAGE 40)

1. window in door now round; 2. rag missing from trash can; 3. hubcap different; 4. wrench got smaller; 5. shadow on hood elongated; 6. cap turned around; 7. wrench head added; 8. cord got shorter; 9. hanging parts missing; 10. coffee mug vanished; 11. workstation drawer altered; 12. wires missing; 13. screwdriver rolled away; 14. tread pattern different; 15. cord from overhead light missing

WITNESS STATEMENTS (PAGE 41)

Mr. Jones lives in House D.

SLITHERLINK PATH (PAGE 42)

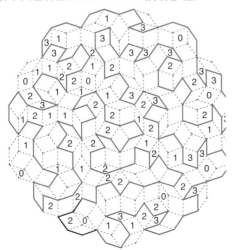

KNOT PROBLEM (PAGE 43)

C is knotted.

QUIPU (PAGE 43)

C

SPY FLY (PAGE 44)

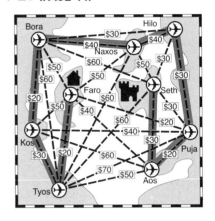

FIND THE SUSPECT (PAGE 45)

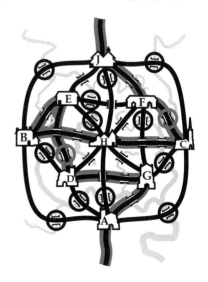

ANSWERS

LATIN (PAGES 46-47)

The leftover letters spell: "Latin is used on tombstones because it is a dead language."

FINGERPRINT MATCH (PAGE 48)

is the matching fingerprint.

WHAT DO YOU SEE? (PAGES 49-50)

cture 1 is a match.

HIGH FIVES (PAGE 51)

Name	Surname	Subject	University
Daisy	Gopher	history	MIT
Ben	Jelly	physics	Caltech
Arnold	Harris	philosophy	Yale
Ellen	Fate	mathematics	Harvard
Cathy	Ink	economics	Princeton

DRESSING ROOM (PAGE 52)

1. bench post added; 2. helmet design shorter; 3. helmet air vent gone; 4. helmet circle wiped away; 5. post behind bench vanished; 6. third strip of tape added to stick; 7. glove design gone; 8. glove short a finger; 9. puck removed; 10. shin guard square gone; 11. design on shin guard vanished; 12. skate pattern altered; 13. lace missing; 14. skate different; 15. knee pad altered

GAME BOARD (PAGES 53-54)

ANSWERS

WORD TRIO (PAGE 55)

WORD TRIO (PAGE 55)

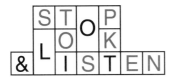

ACROSTIC (PAGES 56-57)

A. shawl; B. unencumbered; C. sheaf; D. mysteriously; E. rattlesnake; F. oaths; G. honeymooners; H. adrenaline

"Make yourself an honest man, and then you may be sure there is one less rascal in the world."

CRACK THE CODE (PAGE 58)

D. The sequence consist of the repeated symbols:

CRACK THE CODE (PAGE 58)

Roseate. The middle 3 letters of each word spell out the Ernest Hemingway novel *The Old Man and the Sea*: hoTHEad, scOLDed, roMANce, abANDon, baTHErs, roSEAte

RIDDLE (PAGE 59)

Alice drove the car down the driveway in reverse.

WORD LADDER (PAGE 59)

Answers may vary. PASS, pars, wars, ward, WORD

INVESTIGATOR'S KIT (PAGES 60-61)

HOT UNDER THE COLLAR (PAGE 62)

What did the arsonist say to his sweetheart? C'mon, baby, light my fire.

SCIENCE WINS! (PAGE 62)

forensic evidence

MOTEL HIDEOUT (PAGE 63)

The thief is in room 28.

THE BODY FARM (PAGES 64-66)

1. False. 2. True. 3. True. 4. True. 5. False

WHAT DO YOU SEE (PAGES 67-68)

Picture 3 is a match.

ANSWERS

QUICK CRIME QUIZ (PAGE 69)

. How to tell drowning from strangulation. 2. 800s. 3. 1980s. 4. 1900s. 5. 1908.

ALL SECRET PLOTS LEAVE CLUES (PAGE 70)

nswers may vary. PLOTS, slots, slits, flits, es, flues, CLUES

A CASE OF ARSON (PAGE 70)

nswers may vary. FIRE, dire, dirt, dart, cart, ast, CASE

IDENTITY PARADE (PAGE 71)

A   B   C   D

KNOWNS AND UNKNOWNS (PAGES 72-74)

Possibly true. If Hrupington did take the ptop to the conference, and it is now miss-g from the hotel room, it seems likely that e murderer did take the laptop. However, the counts of the roommate and boyfriend cast me doubt on this. 2. This seems unlikely. hile the laptop may have been stolen, other luables such as jewelry and smartphone were t behind. 3. Possibly true. While we do know t Hrupington withdrew $80 from an ATM the Wednesday before the murder, it could ve been spent prior to the murder. 4. This ems likely, as they did not belong to Hrup-ton. 5. False. Hrupington attended a panel day afternoon.

FINGERPRINT MATCH (PAGE 75)

The matching pairs are: A and M; B and G; C and P; D and K; E and J; F and O; H and I; L and N

WITNESS STATEMENTS ((PAGES 76-78)

Thursday, 8 PM: Hrupington checks into hotel; Thursday, 10 PM: Hrupington visits hotel bar; Friday, 9 AM: Freesia Jones sees Hrupington outside their rooms; Friday, 2 PM: Hrupington at mulch panel; Friday, 4 PM: Hrupington attends rose panel; Friday, 6:30 PM: Hrupington attends dinner at hotel restaurant; Friday, 8 PM: Hrup-ington leaves restaurant; Friday, 9 PM: Smith hears movement in room next to his (Hrupington's) Bonus answer: Waxman, the moderator of the mulch panel, said he had first spoken to her at the mulch panel on Friday, but the waitstaff identified him as one of the people to speak to Hrupington at the hotel bar on Thursday night.

EAVESDROPPING LOGIC (PAGE 79)

The answer is D. It is not clear, as in A, that both women are upset. While B is true accord-ing to the first woman, it is not clear from both women's comments. C is not clear, as we don't know there is as much at stake as this (or that they are, in fact, friends with the woman).

CRACK THE PASSWORD (PAGE 79)

O
The Greatest Show on Earth

MIXED-UP MARRIAGES (PAGE 80)

	Groom 1st	Groom 2nd	Bride 1st	Bride 2nd
1	Eddie	Kite	Nina	Tallis
2	Bill	James	Rosie	Wells
3	Abe	Goliath	Pauline	Underwood
4	Fred	Holderness	Olive	Stephens
5	Doug	Idi	Alice	Yates
6	Colin	Leonard	Minnie	Vitori

ANSWERS

TAILGATE PARTY (PAGE 81)

1. woman moved left; 2. same woman holding bottle instead of cup; 3. cook wearing shorts; 4. chain missing from tailgate; 5. bottles missing from cooler; 6. cap is now forward; 7. soda missing from man's hand; 8. only one burger on the grill; 9. stadium in background different; 10. license plate "4" now "U."

WITNESS STATEMENTS (PAGE 82)

Mr. Linus lives in House E.

MOTEL HIDEOUT (PAGE 83)

The thief is in room 45.

MASTER OF SUSPENSE (PAGES 84–85)

H	O	R	N	■	M	E	D	A	L	■	I	N	I	T
I	C	E	E	■	I	N	I	G	O	■	N	E	R	O
T	H	E	L	A	D	Y	V	A	N	I	S	H	E	S
S	O	D	■	I	R	A	E	■	G	N	E	I	S	S
■	■	■	C	S	I	■	■	U	O	F	A	■	■	■
S	P	E	L	L	B	O	U	N	D	■	M	A	S	S
A	R	G	U	E	■	S	L	I	D	■	H	E	T	■
B	O	R	E	■	W	A	T	T	S	■	D	E	E	R
E	T	E	■	O	G	R	E	■	M	I	A	T	A	■
R	O	T	C	■	R	E	A	R	W	I	N	D	O	W
■	■	O	D	D	S	■	■	I	D	E	■	■	■	■
N	A	R	R	O	W	■	A	L	E	G	■	B	A	G
T	H	E	P	A	R	A	D	I	N	E	C	A	S	E
W	O	E	S	■	A	M	O	R	E	■	E	S	P	N
T	Y	K	E	■	P	A	G	E	R	■	L	E	S	T

IDENTITY PARADE (PAGE 86)

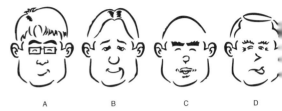

A   B   C   D

WHERE DOES ARSON FIT? (PAGE 87)

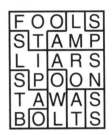

FIND THE SUSPECT (PAGE 88)

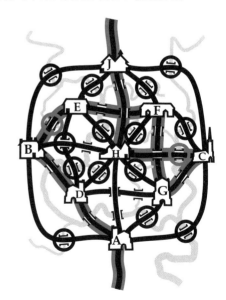

ANSWERS

CHEMICAL REACTION (PAGE 89)

. We know the first chemical (Chem1) and the
second chemical (Chem2) will total 40 ounces.
We also know that 40 ounces times $70 is
2,800.

o:

Chem1 + Chem2 = 40
0 X Chem1 + 40 X Chem2 = 2800
Multiply the first equation by -90.
90 Chem1 -90 Chem2 = -3600
0 Chem1 + 40 Chem2 = 2800
0 Chem 2 = -800
Chem2 equals 16 ounces, which means
Chem1 = 24 ounces

NUMBER SEQUENCE (PAGE 89)

094. Each successive number is 3 times larger
than the number immediately preceding it
minus one. Add each number in the sequence
complete the pattern.

SHROUDED SUMMARY

(PAGES 90-91)

ying tycoon hires
detective for black-
mail case, which
becomes entwined
th scandals involv-
g both daughters.
he Big Sleep" by
aymond Chandler

```
S T H P Y J Q A B O U L A
D Y I N G F L U S F L I N
A C R K B L C M I L D U H
T O E V I T C E T E D E R
S O S F R T C N O Y B E
C N M E S D E T T V O E C
H I R D F S W E S B R W H
C H B O H T H C L D Y H K
I G N I V O I A L V N G I
W I H Y T W C S C A E S E
N T W N D K H E I E S C A
N D S E M O C E B A L S B
L A C A N K M D A F O T Y
B C I D E T H I W I H B O
T L H D Y G W I T H I V O
L V I G W T H I I C S Q P
E W U I M S C A N D A L S
H E I E S C A X V E B K J
A N F R L D H T O B D Q M
B K M L W H T C L L A H D
H I R D F S W E V J U L K
F H I S T W D E I B G C B
M I L D U H N I N M H D S
B C O M L B S T G J T I B
M U S I M P I C E D E R E
S I S T N S E D E L R A C
E O U E R M O U L N S A R
```

PICTURE THIS (PAGE 92)

BACK UP YOUR MEMORY (PAGE 94)

Backboard; backpack, back flip, backgammon

GLOBE QUEST (PAGE 95)

1. Miami	41
2. New York	51
3. Denver	63
4. Phoenix	52
5. Los Angeles	32
6. Chicago	45
7. Atlanta	20
8. Dallas	34
9. Seattle	
TOTAL	338

CRACK THE CODE (PAGE 96)

◆ = 2   ● = 3   ❑ = 4   ❋ = 5

◯ = 6   ✳ = 7   ❖ = 8   ❄ = 10

ANSWERS

SEEN AT THE SCENE (PAGES 97–98)
Santa, elf, snowman, reindeer, sleigh bell

CANDY SHOP (PAGE 99)
Anne Hall, gum balls, $1.25
Denise Page, Swedish fish, $1.00
Monica Smith, licorice, $1.75
Sally Jones, chocolate, $1.50

In the description below, each number in parentheses refers to the clue number that the preceding statement is derived from:
Since Ms. Hall spent 25 cents more than the girl who bought the Swedish fish and 50 cents less than Monica (4), Monica must have spent $1.75 and Ms. Hall spent $1.25 while $1.00 was spent by the girl who bought the Swedish fish. Since Sally's last name is Jones but she didn't buy the Swedish fish (5), by elimination she must have spent $1.50 on candy. Since Denise's last name isn't Hall (1), by elimination she must have bought the Swedish fish. Therefore also by elimination, Anne's last name is Hall. Anne also bought gum balls (2). Since Anne spent less than the girl whose last name is Smith (2), by elimination Monica's last name must be Smith and Denise's last name is Page. Monica didn't buy chocolate (1), so by elimination Monica bought licorice and Sally bought chocolate.

FORENSIC CAREERS (PAGES 100–101)

CRIME RHYMES (PAGE 102)
1. Fry alibi; 2. lyre fire; 3. steeplechase case;
4. melon felon; 5. knock hemlock; 6. supplied cyanide; 7. gem mayhem; 8. mortician suspicion

PERFECT PAIRS (PAGE 102)
seen, scene

MOTEL HIDEOUT (PAGE 103)
The thief is in room 32.

FINGERPRINT MATCH (PAGE 104)
C, F, and I are matches.

WHAT DO YOU SEE? (PAGES 105–106)
1. D; 2. B; 3. No; 4. Yes

ANSWERS

EAVESDROPPING LOGIC (PAGE 107)

The answer is A, as the idea that nobody "could" have heard her suggests that she is denying the accusation, and the idea that nobody "would" have heard it suggests a condition under which it would not have happened, perhaps implying a sentence in which the woman defends the fact that she overheard something. Whereas "should" suggests that it was improper for the conversation to be overheard, and is most compatible with an admission of guilt.

CRACK THE PASSWORD (PAGE 107)

The missing letter is P. The sequence: Life, Liberty, And The Pursuit Of Happiness

WITNESS STATEMENTS (PAGE 108)

Mr. Foreman lives in House A.

DIVE RIGHT IN (PAGE 109)

1. swimmer's reflection is missing; 2. window frame colored in; 3. goggles now have outline; 4. more water above swimmer's head; 5. 2008 now 2009; 6. no and on are swapped on sign; 7. sign missing; 8. swimmer's thumb is missing; 9. wall stripe vanished; 10. water drop below swim meet sign is gone.

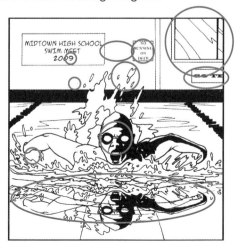

FIND THE SUSPECT (PAGE 110)

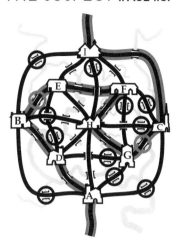

GAME BOARD (PAGES 111-112)

	A	B	C	D	E
1	△	△	△	☆	△
2	○	□	○	○	○
3	☆	☆	☆		☆
4				△	
5	□	○	□	□	□

KNOT PROBLEM (PAGE 113)

Figure A contains 3 unlinked rings of string.

ANAGRAMMAR (PAGE 113)

ALERT

ANAGRAMMAR (PAGE 114)

ARTICLE

TO THE LETTER (PAGE 114)

pursue, purse

ANSWERS

SEEN AT THE SCENE (PAGES 115-116)
Pliers, plane, sawhorse, hammer, hand saw, utility knife

TO THE LETTER (PAGE 117)
fright, fight

KNOT PROBLEM (PAGE 117)
B

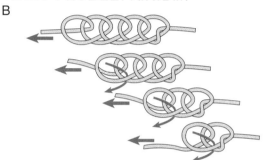

THE RINGMAKER (PAGES 118-119)

Pick-Ups	Customers	Metals	Stones
Monday	Martin	titanium	emerald
Tuesday	Humphrey	platinum	sapphire
Wednesday	George	white gold	amethyst
Thursday	Clark	silver	diamond
Friday	Bernie	yellow gold	ruby

SAY WHAT? (PAGE 120)
"I've always felt that the real horror is next door to us, that the scariest monsters are our neighbors."

CRACK THE PASSWORD (PAGE 120)
The missing letter is S.
INCISOR
OURSELF
PASSION

FIND THE SUSPECT (PAGE 121)

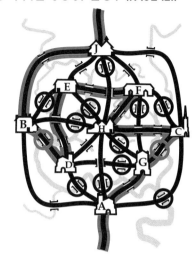

SLITHERLINK PATH (PAGE 122)

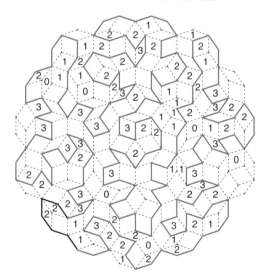

ANSWERS

MISSING DETAILS (PAGE 123)

1. sandal tie/bow; 2. circle design on sleeve; 3. corner design on shield; 4. belt; 5. decorative shirt collar; 6. mouth; 7. sandal strap on the foot; 8. pleat in pants

CLASS SCHEDULE (PAGE 124)

Subject	Teacher	Room
Geography	Irving	E9
Art	Harrison	A2
Chemistry	Jones	F7
English	Kettering	D5
Biology	Lee	C8
History	Gates	B1

TALKING TERMINOLOGY (PAGE 125)

1. B; 2. A describes theft, B describes robbery and C describes burglary. 3. B; 4. Accelerant

REPLICANTS (PAGE 126)

forensic evidence

ADDAGRAM (PAGE 126)

The missing letter is V.
solve, evidence, investigate, detective, thieves

MOTEL HIDEOUT (PAGE 127)

The thief is in room 12.

EAVESDROPPING LOGIC (PAGE 128)

A is untrue. B and C are correct.

EAVESDROPPING LOGIC (PAGE 128)

The answer is B. Although we know that John is certain about this, we don't know how certain the others are (or feel), just that they are in disagreement. On the other hand we can be fairly sure that A, C, and D are reasonable. A must be true for there to be such disagreement between Barbara and Carol. C must be true from our point of view, as we don't know the details of the situation, nor who is right in their opinions. D is clearly also true.

IT'S IN THE BLOOD (PAGES 129-130)

1. A+; 2. O-; 3. AB+; 4. AB-; 5. True

WITNESS STATEMENT (PAGE 131)

Mr. Stark lives in House D.

KNOT PROBLEM (PAGE 132)

KNOT PROBLEM (PAGE 132)

C would knot up.

ANSWERS

GAME BOARD (PAGES 133-134)

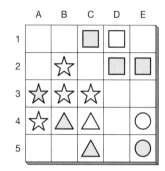

SYMBOLS OF OZ (PAGES 135-136)
Kangaroo, boomerang, Australian flag, emu, koala, Ayers Rock

CANVASS THE BUILDING (PAGE 137)

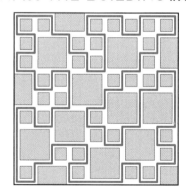

CRACK THE PASSWORD (PAGE 138)
The missing letter is U.
COSTUME
DURABLE
FORMULA
HIRSUTE

CRACK THE PASSWORD (PAGE 138)
The missing letter is T.
TEMPERA
TESTIFY
TRILOGY

WHAT DO YOU SEE? (PAGES 139-140)
1. False; 2. 4; 3; False; 4. True; 5. False

QUICK CRIME QUIZ (PAGE 141)
1. No. They may have been there but worn gloves, for example. 2. No. A body farm describes a place where forensic investigators te to see what happens to corpses under differer conditions. 3. Yes. 4. Yes. Many courts do not admit polygraph evidence, because they can show both false negatives and false positives. 5. Automated Fingerprint Identification System

A CASE OF ARSON (PAGES 142-144)
1. Unlikely. Turpentine was used as an accelerant, and it was not stored in the office. 2. False. 3. Unconfirmed. Greene had returned th keycard issued by the company, but he could have duplicated it prior to leaving. 4. True, his girlfriend. 5. Unconfirmed, as the only word fo this was his own.

AFTERNOON ICE CREAM (PAGE 145)
Emily, sundae, coffee
Helen, cone, chocolate
Sally, frappe, vanilla
In the explanation below, each number in parentheses refers to the clue number that the preceding statement is derived from:
Sally ordered a frappe (4). Since she didn't get chocolate ice cream (4) and the one that got coffee ice cream also ordered a sundae (3), by elimination Sally got vanilla ice cream. Emily didn't order an ice cream cone (1) so by elimination she must have ordered the sundae Therefore by elimination, Helen ordered the cone with chocolate ice cream.

Name	Ordered	Flavor
EMILY	SUNDAE	COFFEE
HELEN	CONE	CHOCOLATE
SALLY	FRAPPE	VANILLA

ANSWERS

SHE'S A COP! (PAGES 146-147)

```
C T M D N R E L T O T I C E W
L S H P O L E J S D I O L I P
R A A G W M H S R C D A T W O
P C W T I O I S O A C H U I L
I O Q A O S V S U L O S E T I
S H L K N S N Q S U C C O S C
T H E I P D S I T I A E C O E
E R C I C D O A A R N G H U W
P S A P O E T R G L S G T T R
O E A M H R W G D P P W H M T
L H E C A O N O U E Q N E I H
I H W C D I L C M O R C I S O
T C E H V L T J H A N S A S U
I I I A I C O T E C N S V I S
A C S L N P L C W I T H O U W
```

HOCKEY LEGENDS (PAGES 148-149)

Autograph Price	Player	Booth Number	Photo Price
$10	Uri Ulner	booth #7	$20
$15	Rick Rogers	booth #6	$75
$25	Chip Caitlin	booth #12	$55
$35	Dan Dalton	booth #3	$40
$50	Jim Janelle	booth #10	$30

FINGERPRINT MATCH (PAGE 150)

H is the matching fingerprint.

PLANTED EVIDENCE AT THE SCENE (PAGE 151)

Answers may vary. PLANT, slant, scant, scent, SCENE

ELEVATOR WORDS (PAGE 151)

1. CRIME wave; 2. waveform; 3. form letter; 4. letterhead; 5. headband; 6. band music; 7. music SCENE

ON YOUR MARK, GET SET . . . (PAGE 152)

1. hair color is different; 2. wristband is missing; 3. railing post added; 4. stripe on shorts erased; 5. socks have fewer stripes; 6. facial hair missing; 7. track has extra lane; 8. runner's number added a 1; 9. "team" spelled "teem"; 10. shoes changed color

PLAYMAKER (PAGES 153-154)

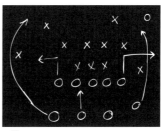

5.

ANSWERS

GAME BOARD (PAGES 155-156)

	A	B	C	D	E
1	☆				◼
2		◼	○		
3				☆	
4		●			
5	△				△

CRACK THE PASSWORD (PAGE 157)

The missing letter is X.
EXPLAIN
EXPLODE
EXPRESS

CRACK THE PASSWORD (PAGE 157)

The missing letter is V.
ARCHIVE
PRIVACY
REVERIE

ROYAL CARTOGRAPHERS (PAGES 158-159)

Careers	Cartographers	Map Areas	Auction Prices
1624-1645	Gaulois	Americas	$273,000
1645-1652	Dupuys	Europe	$144,000
1652-1676	Irinaise	Asia	$125,000
1676-1680	Laliane	Africa	$85,000
1680-1691	Penstrent	World	$116,000

CRACK THE CODE (PAGE 160)

▢ = 1   ◯ = 3   ● = 4   ❄ = 5

✳ = 6   ❖ = 8   ✳ = 9   ▼ = 10

GLOBE QUEST (PAGE 161)

1. Miami — 33
2. Dallas — 28
3. Los Angeles — 54
4. Chicago — 63
5. Atlanta — 41
6. New York — 51
7. Denver — 54
8. Phoenix — 50
9. Seattle

TOTAL — 374

SCIENTISTS (PAGES 162-163)

1. Descartes; 2. Bohr; 3. Pasteur; 4. Copernicus; 5. Planck; 6. Einstein; 7. Newton; 8. da Vinci; 9. Darwin; 10. Archimedes; 11. Franklin; 12. Curie; 13. Kepler; 14. Faraday; 15. Tesla

```
U N I W R A D A V I N C I E W
F A R A D A Y N R L V B S I R
G J V H G L L R I G W E P U U
Q F R C U V I H R E V X U N E
A J P G O H F O W O T R M E T
C D S R T P Z B J V Y S N Q S
P U E N P J E R B B Y E N J A
T N M S O L E R S Z W Y C I P
E I E E C L A A N T W I R I E
S L K U P A R N O I Q R C I L
L K J E N U R N C F C R C S S
A N K V H E L T N K R U J H N
Q A W X Q P F A E Q Q W S K N
S R W K N Y A M U S C U R I E
Q F A R C H I M E D E S I J K
```

ANSWERS

SPY FLY (PAGE 164)

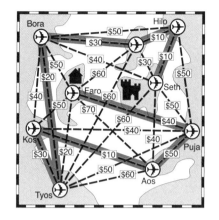

ACRONYM QUIZ (PAGES 165-166)
1. B; 2. C; 3. A; 4. B; 5. A

FIND THE SUSPECT (PAGE 167)

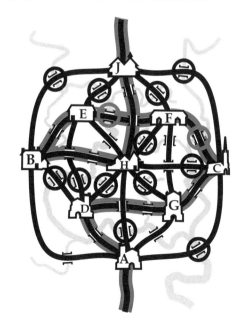

LOCKER ROOM (PAGE 168)
1. locker vent gone; 2. shoulder pads neckline different; 3. shoulder pads missing side panel; 4. lace missing on shoe; 5. design on shoe altered; 6. shin guard different; 7. laces missing on chest protector; 8. marker different; 9. football missing laces. 10. light switch now off; 11. play different on chalkboard; 12. bench bolt disappeared; 13. chalk vanished; 14. wheel rolled away; 15 helmet altered

PRIME SUSPECT (PAGE 169)

	Nationality	Hair	Coat	Build
1	Italian	none	green	round
2	English	red	blue	thin
3	Chinese	gray	purple	slim
4	Spanish	white	cream	medium
5	African	dark	yellow	hunched
6	Mexican	brown	mauve	fat

CURRENCY QUIZ (PAGE 170)
1. b) France
2. a) Switzerland
3. d) Albania
4. a) Paraguay
5. d) Iraq
6. a) United Kingdom
7. b) Bangladesh

ANSWERS

SPY FLY (PAGE 171)

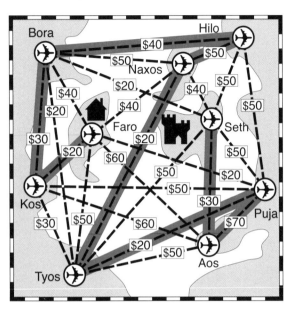

SLITHERLINK PATH (PAGE 174)

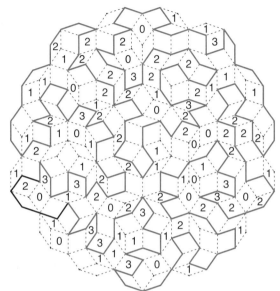

THE LAW (PAGES 172-173)